An Eccentric Story, From This to This

A True Story of Change and Redemption

Jonmarc Dewalt

Absolute Author Publishing House

New Orleans, LA

Absolute Author
Publishing House

Publisher: Absolute Author Publishing House
Editor: Dr. Melissa Caudle
Interior Designer: Dr. Melissa Caudle
Cover Designer: Rebeca @Rebecacovers

ISBN: 978-1-951028-66-4

An Eccentric Story, From This to This/Jonmarc Dewalt

1. Memoir 2. Autobiography

PRINTED IN THE UNITED STATES OF AMERICA

ACKNOWLEDGMENT

My son inspires me the most to be the best that I can be. The following people because of their resilience and tenacity:

My Father

My mother

Shawn Farnum

Ade & Addea Cox

Mark Cuban

Eric Thomas

John H Johnson

DEDICATION

For my family. I dedicate this book to my mother Veronica, my father Wilbert, my sister Lindsay, and my son Joseph.

TABLE OF CONTENT

THE BEGINNING OF MY TROUBLES

Wednesday, January 20th, 1988, at approximately 8:30 p.m., I was pushed out of my mother's womb after she spent hours of intense pain in labor. She is truly a symbol of pure strength and will. My mom, known as Sister V, is one of my first examples of persistence; she displayed this by pushing me into the world in Beth Israel Hospital, located in New York City. It was at that moment the world was impacted forever and would never be the same.

It all started in my early childhood, which was no different from any other kid in the inner city. My parents are hard-working, middle-class citizens. My parents are the epitome of the blue-collar, hardworking, middle class family. Comprised of a voluntary immigrant (my mother) and the descendant of slaves, involuntary immigrants to America (my father's lineage). My mother migrated from Saint Elizabeth, Balaclava, Jamaica to America for a better life at the age of eighteen, having been left behind by my trailblazing grandmother, Hortensia, who came to America to pursue a successful career as a nurse in Brooklyn's Woodhall hospital. She paved the way for my mother to come, who struggled for many years upon her arrival, being diligent and completing her college education at one of the City Universities of New York. On the other hand, my father, who was the descendent of slaves in Texas, came to New York as a child and was raised in Bushwick, Brooklyn. He studied martial arts and was a hardworking real estate agent; he had a formal education as well, however he had to end his college career one semester before matriculating in order to provide for my mother who was pregnant with me.

Before my sister and I were born, they resided in a middle-class neighborhood in Brooklyn, New York. After my birth, my parents realized they had to move to a better community with a larger house to provide us an opportunity to have a backyard. A backyard was considered a luxury, and most families did not have one.

My parents are God-fearing, law-abiding citizens. In fact, as a youth, I questioned why my mother, who was a Jamaican immigrant, and my father, a Brooklyn native whose roots went back to Texas, worked so hard. I mean fifty plus hours a week of hard labor.

As a toddler, many people thought that I was created for a divine purpose. I grew up in a Baptist church where my father was a deacon, and my mother, a senior member. Growing up in church gave me values and a sense of morals, but as you will see, sometimes, we as Christians forget our way. As a youth and latchkey kid, there were many evenings I wanted to play catch with my father at the park; however, his work schedule would not allow for this to happen. His actions frustrated me many times and caused me to wander my neighborhood in search of things to do, sometimes the wrong thing.

Enough whining like a spoiled brat. Compared to the other kids in my neighborhood, I had a pretty good upbringing. Many of my peers came from dysfunctional families raised by a single mother or by grandparents. Others had parents or family members who were either strung out on drugs or sold drugs to earn money. Others were desperate and devised schemes to put food on the table, such as burglarizing or killing people for money. As an example, one of my childhood friend's father murdered a neighbor and stuffed the lady's body in the closet. Another Haitian neighbor shot and killed his mother-in-law because she threatened to tell the police that he was selling cocaine. Seeing and hearing these stories tends to have a tremendous impact on the psyche of a young mind.

GRADE SCHOOL BULLIES

G rowing up in Hollis, Queens on Farmers Boulevard was not an easy thing to do for anyone in that area.

My behavioral problems started in grade school with my teachers and peers. My ability to focus and the immense amount of energy I had compromised my learning and negatively impacted my behavior. I was very hyperactive; I couldn't sit still or concentrate for more than ten minutes. Some might say I suffered from Attention Deficit Hyperactivity Disorder, better known as ADHD. I remember one day in the second grade when I went to the bathroom and smeared the wall with my feces. I know you might be thinking to yourself – this kid is foul and has a few screws missing. Truth be told, I was eccentric, truly different; I viewed that moment as a scientific art meeting curiosity to the extreme.

My parents tried every possible method to give me a chance at a better education and opportunities. Still, my behavioral woes worsened, which became more evident in my primary school years while attending private school. I made a poor choice when I stabbed a female classmate in the ear with a pencil because she told me "no" when I asked for a snack out of her lunch box. I guess I watched too many *Tom and Jerry* cartoons or just too much TV.

In the second grade, where I was enrolled in my third school, the administrator expelled me. I guess it was safe to say that I needed to be placed in a more structured environment. To provide insight, my poor behavior, I believe, stemmed from being bullied a lot at school. I was basically being picked on because my parents worked over fifty hours a week to provide for my sister and me. After all bills and expenses, there was no money left for fancy and trendy urban wear; therefore, that meant wearing the hideous school uniform at the time.

If you were born in the 80s or the late 90s, then you know about the mandates of school uniforms. Let me break it down for you. If you aren't from the inner cities of America and never attended a public school in the ghetto, the uniforms were a bright yellow shirt, somewhat like a bumblebee color, a clip-on, navy-blue tie, and tight, blue church pants from a store called Cookies. As for many of my peers, their parents bought them designer clothes, which consisted of the latest brands such as Nikes, Jordan's, Levi jeans, North Poles jackets, name-brand bags, and the latest ice-burg shirts amongst other fashionable items. You know, the typical urban streetwear, which most kids desired at that time, including me.

If you had a certain kind of book bag, for instance, a JanSport, a Nike sling backpack, or even a North Face bookbag, you were popular and accepted amongst the other kids. Now, I know this sounds a bit frivolous, however, yes, all this fashion-forward dressing was taking place in my grade school amongst adolescents. This type of social hierarchy of order in grade school was the beginning of my social experience and understanding of how kids, or even people, worked. The truth is, I lacked social skills and didn't understand how to interact with others, which made grade school rough for me. I became the laughingstock and was continuously bullied due to my lack of trendy clothes or the know-how to socialize properly.

I know you think this is childish, right? Why should this be a big deal? The truth is it was a big deal. In grade school, kids can be mean and say the darndest and most hurtful things. When they did, it led to a lot of frustration, embarrassment, and ultimately resulted in a lot of fights for me – not your ideal childhood. I can remember many days fighting over simple things such as people making jokes about my mother, because of my name, the way I spoke "properly" or physically harassing me "just because."

My struggles weren't only with my peers, I also had violent conflicts with the teachers. One time, out of anger, I threw a desk at a teacher. The school felt the solution at that point was for me to be assigned to a special education class: therefore, labeled. My parents were desperate; I had been kicked out of several public schools by the time I was eight. I even attended a private school in Harlem, New York, to avoid going into special education.

My parents were referred to someone who could help me. Under the tutelage of a lady named Ms. White, for a whole year, I attended school on the famous 125th street. There, I flirted with girls and had behavioral issues. For example, on a field trip, I destroyed my CD player out of pure rebellion rather than give it to my father or the teacher. That day I indeed showed my ass and embarrassed my father.

As I look back, my father displayed an immense amount of patience. He did not believe that physical abuse or punishments were the solution, but believed that showing me love, kindness, compassion, and patience would help me improve my behavior in the short term and help turn my life around in the future. After that, I was dismissed from that private school without hesitation and returned to public school 134, located in Hollis, Queens, and was placed in a fourth-grade special education class.

After being transferred, my fighting and disruptive behavior continued. The school psychologist became involved at that point and recommended medication after several evaluations. The school psychologist recommended that I take Ritalin. My mother, a wise woman, said, "Hell no, I will not allow you to give drugs to my son."

Although I continued to get into trouble, my mother decided not to allow the school system to put me on medication. I think she made a great choice. To date, it has been scientifically proven that big pharmaceutical companies test those psychosis drugs on troubled youth in the public-school system, which later in life have had numerous social and phycological side effects.

SCHOOL HORROR

From primary school to high school, I was always in trouble; in fact, the bottom line was I couldn't focus with all the bullying and peer pressure around me. I used to get into fights with classmates because we all had the same behavioral issues being that we were placed in special education. This environment didn't help because it created social discrimination among regular students and those in special education classes. We were looked at as inferior or as lesser students who were stupid or retarded.

Being a young boy, with a young mind, and having to deal with all these social pressures which I did not know at the time, negatively impacted me. Imagine riding to school every day on a short yellow bus and being labeled as a special education student or one who had special needs.

I bounced from school to school, completing a circuit of fourteen schools, and two months into the ninth grade, I was expelled for fighting. All my problems worsened once I started hanging out after school in the neighborhood where I was from. At home, I was taught positive things, spirituality, and how to be politically correct. However, outside seemed like a dark, twisted fantasy compared to my upbringing.

Once I left the safety of my home and exited the front gate, the world seemed to be full of despair. The journey between home and school came with many negative influences. In the neighborhood also known across America as "the hood" or to say the least, the inner city, I was introduced to the vices and the dark side of my community. I had to learn to fight and be tough early, because if not you'd fall victim to the streets which were crawling with grimy characters.

Many of my peers were neighborhood friends, or as I like to call them now that I am older and wiser, associates. In fact, some would say we were a gang or a clique. My entire life, my parents and other family members did their best to shelter me from the realities of the hood. Once at school, the different neighborhoods would have what we called rivalries or beefs over silly things. I never knew that trouble could brew after a person looked at someone the wrong way, stared for too long, stepped on someone's shoes, talked to someone else's girlfriend, wore the wrong colors, and ironically, just for growing up on the wrong side of town.

This way of thinking was toxic and did nothing to help those involved in petty and violent crimes. This mentality caused problems that escalated into all-out fights, shootouts, and stabbings on a countless number of occasions.

To elaborate a bit more, if you were caught after school with the wrong crowd, for instance, you would be guilty by association. Many times, kids ended up committing robberies, getting into fights, and loitering on the street corners of the neighborhoods. Chaos is the first word that comes to mind as I look back, in retrospect, among the many days, weeks, and years spent hanging out with the people from my neighborhood. Those interactions led me to get into brawls and get jumped by rival cliques or even arrested for juvenile offenses.

The first time police officers detained me was at Louis Armstrong Middle School in Corona, Queens. The bigger kid, who was from South Jamaica, Queens, teased me. His name was Gustavo, and he kept antagonizing and making fun of me for some strange reason. So, at the end of the school period, he approached me, and I then went for his hand. I bent his finger back until I heard it snap while everyone watched. I didn't think of the consequences, but I knew that I was tired of being bullied. More importantly, my parents could have been sued and lost everything, which I didn't understand until my mother whipped me with an extension cord as if I were a slave and yelled that sentiment out.

A pattern would, unfortunately, start, whereas I was arrested for juvenile offenses such as the above incident. I was given a juvenile card since I was too young to go to jail. I was twelve, and I couldn't be arrested. However, I received the superintendent suspension for breaking this kids' hand and was then kicked out of that school – thus starting the trend. I was kicked out and placed in an alternative school and then sent to Intermediate School 238 or Susan B. Anthony in Jamaica, New York on Hillside Avenue. I was always in constant trouble because I spoke my mind, even if it got me into problems. I remember one time cursing out a young lady, Unique, in art class and telling her to screw her mother because she kept teasing me. Then she called her brothers to the school to beat me up. I also had numerous fights, including one where I fought twin brothers from Woodhull. I beat them up at the same time.

My school was so bad. I remember one day I was robbed at gunpoint by some guys who didn't even attend the school from the opposite side of town; nothing happened, thank God. I succumbed and gave them whatever they wanted, which was nothing except a few dollars.

Later, the administration expelled me for using a wrestling move called the Rock bottom, slamming a random kid onto the ground. Let me be clear. The kid didn't do anything to me. His only error that day was walking in the hall across my path. However, my dean at the time was a gentleman named Mr. Sean Farnum. He was somewhat of a mentor; however, I didn't realize it at the time because I was a young knucklehead. He had no choice but to expel me. I will add that he was very disappointed by my actions, as was Ms. Wiggins, the school superintendent.

I then went to another school called Intermediate School 59, where things only spiraled downhill; my behavior got worse. I was now fourteen, about to turn fifteen, and labeled a knucklehead or troublemaker by everyone. I received many lectures, "You're not only battling with peer pressure; you're battling with puberty, your first girlfriend or boyfriend, hormones, and the expectations of your family."

So, for me, I was a young knucklehead, unfortunately, with a reputation from other schools and in the neighborhood. This created instant tension with my new teachers and with other students who were from the west side of Merrick and me being from Farmers Boulevard or Farmers bully as they called it. This was a recipe for trouble and bad things.

While I was attending I.S. 59, the final straw was when I punched a girl in the face because she was fighting one of my female associates. At this junction, school administrators gave me detention, timeouts, mediation, psychotherapy, superintendent suspensions, and all the possible counseling remedies and punishments they could dish.

For being so disruptive, it was my worst week ever as a youth. First, my father was at home. While at home, on an indefinite superintendent suspension for hitting the girl in the face, I ran out of the house, cursing my father in the process and heading to another school called I.S. 192. Why was I so determined? I needed to follow up on a claim that my associate told me about someone bullying him. Thus, the problem was my neighborhood friend said that a group of people from the other side of the boulevard violated him and disrespected him by throwing a snowball at him. So, I found myself being the tough guy in the situation and saw myself as the defender. With my pocketknife concealed in my pocket, I mobilized and rode my bike for fifteen minutes to that school in Hollis, Queens in search of the culprits.

When I arrived, I joined other youths from my neighborhood. In the blink of an eye, when we saw the other group of kids, we commenced into an all-out brawl with those kids from Murdock. The reason I say kids is that's what we all were, lost kids fighting over concrete pride and street signs that didn't even belong to us. It was all something so frivolous and much to do about nothing. Before I continue, let me share some insight in my mind in retrospect.

As I express these experience's it has caused me to think about why I was so angry or frustrated, I believe it was due to being disciplined at home physically due to my family's religious beliefs.

It also stemmed from the frustration of not fitting in, which is the struggle many youths have.

I made one of the poorest decisions in my life while fighting; I remember one of the kids, whom I later identified as Jason, had a steak knife. I wrestled him to the ground and took it from him. Another kid and I somehow found ourselves in a face-off or duel with knives. In the haste of adrenaline, I threw my weapon and ran, not realizing that the several jabs I had taken at this individual with my weapon had struck him in his chest. I never ran so fast in my life.

As I ran, hopping over fences and running past people for blocks at a time, it took me 30 minutes to run straight back to my neighborhood. The police cars sped past me as I ran in the direction of the assault which I had just committed. I finally reached my neighborhood, or the block as we called it, and linked up with my cronies or, better yet, nowadays, my associates. Some thought it would be funny to claim the kid had died, but in reality, the only thoughts running through my head were, *Did I kill him, or is he dead?* What a cruel joke to pull. Deep down, I knew I would be facing life in prison for murder over something so petty, over my pride, my anger, and being ultimately a follower and not a leader in the right context.

Days passed, which felt like months. Every time my doorbell rang, I thought it was the police. After a week went by, I thought I was in the clear and created an illusion that nothing would come of this situation; boy, was I wrong. The streets were talking, and not before long, a detective from the N.Y.P.D. left his business card at my house. Weeks after that, I was arrested and detained for assault with a deadly weapon, among other charges.

I remember sitting in the police station writing a statement about all that had transpired that day while my mother sat next to me, crying in disbelief. The court case would take months to play out and concluded nearly a year later.

Throughout the process, my parents stayed faithful, and even though the world saw their son as a walking time bomb or a violent kid or even worse, a crazy young thug, they believed in me. Also, the psychologist deemed my mother and me crazy due to an analogy that we both concluded that throwing a rock at a squirrel was okay.

GOING INTO THE SLAMMER

During the months leading up to the trial, the judge allowed me to return to school. However, old habits die hard, and without fail, I went to high school. Like I said earlier, that process did not end well, and after the first few weeks, which were topped off with fighting and lack of discipline to attend classes, I took a turn for the worse.

I cut class many days, started smoking marijuana, ran the hallways, hung out with the cool kids, and even found myself receiving oral sex in the stairwells from loose girls. This didn't last long because thereafter, I was expelled from school for getting into a fight I had during school orientation. This meant I disobeyed the judge, and now juvenile detention was going to be my new place of residence.

The first of many destinations was in Astoria, Queens. This place was filled with more ignorant, angry, mentally lost, and violent youth. More importantly, it was also operated by staff workers who should have been locked up themselves. Chaos prevailed, and the workers pretty much allowed the youth to run the house while the workers ran errands, talked on the phone, and sometimes even slept on the job.

To make matters worse, the youth made the rules, which made the environment very contentious. Staff looked the other way while fights happened. In the following months, my case would be sent to trial. On the day it began, I was led into the courtroom, shackled from my waist, hands, and feet. The family courtroom in Queens, New York, was arranged where the victim, Korean Ortiz, for the record would testify to me stabbing him twice. He eventually graphically explained in full, vivid detail what transpired that terrifying day.

I was very remorseful, and thrilled that at the same time, he was still alive. It was a miracle, the doctor explained, that he survived such an attack. The knife blade struck him in the chest and was within centimeters of his heart and, in other words, within centimeters of killing him. And to think this was over something so small and ridiculous. Stupid, really!

After the trial, I left the courtroom straight to Spafford Juvenile Detention – a dumping ground for New York City's worst juveniles. A lot was going on inside, and it was plagued by fights, abuse, and even vermin. And to think, this was where I would spend several months before being transferred to the custody of the state.

In the process, I got into more fights out of anger because if I didn't, I would be labeled as soft and become a target. One Thanksgiving, I had an exchange of words with a member of the Bloods gang, a guy from the Bronx who had cornrows, kind of ugly fellow. After that, as we walked from the mess hall, he was a coward and assaulted me from behind; however, I must give credit to where credit is due. He must have knocked some sense into me that day when he hit me so hard that my head bounced off a metal door.

I had plenty of fights while in the joint. One day in the classroom, over a petty dispute, I beat a kid down who found himself talking stuff. In there, it was the breeding ground for all the troubled youth locked up in this Juvenile Institution. In one case, the staff worker slapped me on my back for coming out of the shower without a shirt on and then hinted that he would tell all the kids to fight me if I dared to challenge or to fight back.

The weeks following, I was sent to the state for transport up north. As I waited in the facility in the Bronx, I had a fight that began with me smacking a kid named Casiano from Brooklyn; we were both restrained for fighting. Throughout my stay, my parents came to visit me, and even my pastor, Arnaldo Campbell, came to wish me farewell. I was transferred to the Upstate New York facility, which took several hours to ride shackled from my feet and handcuffed at the waist, from head to toe. I realized that I was a troubled youth full of rebellious and defiant behavior from the inner city.

When I arrived on that cold, winter evening to the Upstate New York Reformatory village in the city of South Kortright, I felt I would be in for a harsh and rude awakening. The place was called the Allen residential facility and was hidden in the woods which reminded me of the surroundings in the Friday the 13th horror film. My mind was full of more anger and resentment, I blamed my parents, I blamed everyone for me ending up there. I never claimed responsibility.

Once at Allen residential facility, I decided to continue my rebellious behavior. I will never forget what happened next. A staff member who happened to be a burly White man over 300 pounds and six feet, two inches tall told me to go to my room when I tried to use the phone without asking. This turned out to be one of the worst decisions I could have made. He told me to go back to my room twice, verbal warnings I should have heeded, and I yelled and flexed back at him, in my stature I stated, "I don't have to listen to you."

He immediately commenced to place me in a full Nelson wrestling-like maneuver and slammed my face into the carpet-covered ground and then slid me across the floor. During this process of having this man on top of me squeezing, he successfully made me piss in my pants, and then I passed out under the stress of his maneuver. It felt like an eternity; however, after being restrained, a few pieces of my facial tissue were gone.

I learned later that I had suffered severe rug burns and passed out. I was sent to my room and then to the hospital to be taken care of for my wounds. By the way, this is all legal for the state to do as you are the property of the state. Well, if things couldn't get any worse, I was then transferred across the street to a higher-level facility called the sergeant Henry Johnson Youth Leadership Academy, which was the military school for the hardest to deal with kids across New York State.

I attended the "YLA" for thirteen months, and many of the days I was yelled at, physically restrained several times, and reprimanded. I also saw many abuses by the staff, such as when a cadet, Sykes, was given one minute to shower and then was rushed out naked in front of all to see in the dormitory.

This place, I must admit, would be very pivotal in my life. I had a teacher by the name of Mrs. Armstrong who helped me to obtain my GED on the first go-around. She gave a shit, and this encouraged me as well as many other young brothers to achieve our diplomas.

There were many other staff members, or gentlemen, especially one guy by the name of Sergeant Louche who always encouraged us as young men to do better. I remember one day Sergeant Louche saying, "DeWalt, you're going to be all right."

However, I also remember another sergeant by the name of Sergeant Piyanka, a White asshole who stated to me one day, "You'll be back. We'll leave the lights on for you."

I don't know if he was trying to challenge me mentally or just being a seriously negative asshole, but the day I was leaving to go home, unfortunately he was right. I continued down the road of incarceration as an adult. I became involved in situation after situation. Also, in and out of the hoosegow for petty crimes such as theft, fighting, and lastly, at the age of eighteen, I was found guilty for assault stemming from a situation where I resisted arrest.

After that, I was sent back and forth to court for several years until finally, my settlement to the crime of assault in the second-degree wound was handed down. I was sentenced to two years in New York State Prison and charged as an adult for my offenses. During the duration of my process of going to court, I was afraid of the reality of going to prison. I didn't want my freedom taken away and be removed once again from my family. I did not want to be alone. Who was to blame for this? Me, of course; I was taught and warned throughout all of my adolescence and youth to behave, stay out of trouble, don't leave the yard, stay away from certain individuals, and if you see trouble run the other way. My grandma Hansen used to say, "Keep your nose clean and stay out of trouble."

One day, my neighbor told me to specifically to stay away from these two individuals called the Chalmers Brothers. These brothers were two individuals who would show me later in life find out what my neighbor meant by staying away from these men, and those like them meant, but it would be too late.

I also received warnings from other wise people, such as my neighbor, Mr. Curtis, who also told me a great revelation. He said, "Once you're in the system, the legal system is like getting caught in a spider web. Once you're in, you can't get out."

On my way to prison, I was faced with the reality of thinking about where I went wrong AGAIN. I resisted an arrest, which led to an assault, by law, due to the officer's injuries, which he testified that I hurt his shoulder while trying to arrest me. I am sure you're wondering what exactly transpired that day between me, a young African minority male, and two White officers. Simply put, I had gotten into a violent altercation with the owners of the corner store around the corner from my house. I went into the store and tried to steal several bags of potato chips. I know, at seventeen I should have known better, right? Wrong! I was just as ignorant and rude as ever. I was then chased out of the store by the owner, who wielded a machete. I then, in my state of anger and ignorance, found the biggest rock that I could, and I threw it through the store owner's van window.

Fast forward, in retrospect, to my altercation with the police officers. Several days later, I was on the street corner of Farmers Boulevard and Megan Avenue with some old heads waiting to buy several grams of marijuana to flip for a quick few bucks. Then the cops rolled up and told me, "You fit the description of someone who had a gun. Do you mind if we search you?"

It was two White officers, one fat guy, and a skinny White lady. Later on in life, I discovered that the police tactic used is a typical law enforcement line of reverse psychology. It was a lie that I "fit the description of having a gun." They searched me and did not find a gun. They proceeded to handcuff me. At this point, I became irate, belligerent, and very angry. I tried to stop them from cuffing me, and a tussle ensued with the officers taking aggressive actions and using force. For the record, I never fought back, meaning I never threw a single punch or kick.

Thereafter, while subdued and lying on the ground, I was kicked in the head and body several times. I couldn't see them because I had been hit in the eyes by the correctional officers pepper spray, this shit burned my eyes and my soul. As I lay on the ground, I felt helpless; however, I knew that this was all the result of my social choices and interactions with my fellow citizens. This epiphany wouldn't take place until several years later while conducting a session of introspection inside of a prison cell, regarding the latter. However, regarding that night, had I not been arrested, I would have more than likely been gunned down and probably killed that night due to numerous incidents that happened throughout my teenage years leading up to that moment.

Leading up to that night, I had been accused of shooting a boy named Cocky. The reality was that some individuals were seeking revenge in the form of me dying in a hail of gunfire. The truth is I didn't pull the trigger, but I did find myself, unfortunately, involved in that incident. Me being a defender of my so-called friends, led to an incident, which was a fight that broke out at a party where I stomped the dude out because he, or they, were fighting my so-called friends now turned enemies. However, at this point, I found myself back in the hands of the criminal justice system, and off I went to jail.

My mother was hurt. My father, family members, and close friends once they heard the news, made a lot of sacrifices. My parents even put their house up to post my bond. For two years, I found myself going back and forth to court in an ongoing legal battle regarding that arrest. It was during this time I realized that I had no real friends in the streets and that everyone was out to get me. More importantly, I made real strides to grow up fast and not be killed for something I didn't do.

Getting my life together would be the only other option besides death; unfortunately, so would prison at that point. During that time in 2007, I took shortcuts home out of paranoia. Like many other occasions, I found myself numerous times being followed and watched by strange folks. Life got so crazy that my own homeboy, at least that's what I thought, by the name of Donald Vegas, tried to gun me down as I walked along 188th Street one night. I remember him running and wielding a 380 handgun that night. How do I know, you may ask? Because he was that close before I got my "Forest Gump" on and ran. My heart pounded out of my chest, for the first-time death was at my heals, my life flashed before my eyes, it was a scary moment that I was living through once again. Imagine a friend turning into a Judas and trying to take your life, someone you trust, this would create trust issues that exist until this day.

However, I would escape to the barbershop, where I found some help. You can call me what you want, but one thing you can't call me is stupid. In the streets, people are labeled "pussy" or "soft," but once you're dead, that's it, you're dead! As someone who was smart and outgunned like myself at that time, how could I go up against someone else who had a gun? It was a setup at that point, and I realized quickly that a break from this environment was truly needed, although it felt like jumping from one burning building onto another.

PRISON LIFE

P rison life was going to be my only way to escape the madness of the streets and my past. At least that's what I thought – wishful thinking. After being sentenced on February 14th, 2008, to two years in state prison for assault in the second degree, which was a Class D Felony on a police officer, I began to rethink some of my choices. This sentencing revolved around the shoulder injury the policeman testified I gave him, which in my opinion, probably came from the massive amount of punches thrown by the White female police officer.

However, although the injury was not sustained from me throwing a fist, which I never did, I was still charged. It was better than taking my chances with a public defender, going to trial and possibly getting hit with a maximum of seven years in prison. So, there I was at eighteen going on nineteen, and for the second time in my life incarcerated. Before I reached the custody of the state, I had to go to Rikers Island first. Remember, I thought jail would be the best option to get away from my problems in the streets? Well, as soon as I got to the bookings (the holding cell), the henchmen of this guy by the nickname of Cocky was there waiting for me – here we go again another enemy waiting for me in a jail cell. He was sent to remind me that I hadn't escaped the streets and the blood revenge that was being sought. We had one of the most eerie conversations; the conversation ended basically with 'I am going to try to fatally harm you when I get the chance.' I thought to myself, when will this end, its either kill or be killed especially heading to the state penitentiary. I continued thinking of other strange foes I encountered on the streets. The enemy across from me I'll never forget was an older gentleman from Southside Jamaica, Queens. He was a truly cold and bitter guy; he disclosed to me that he had been shot in the head at a young age, the ugly scar was nasty as it sat in clear view on his head. He told me his story, and he was bitter from that situation of being blazingly shot in the housing projects. He had no excuse to live, he was angry and hopeless; I could see why he had no choice but to accept being a goon or killer for money.

I knew this goon and this other older guy I had seen stalking me once before on the street were up to a devious plot. He walked around with a metal foot brace which I truly believed had a knife in it, how else could you clear the metal detectors with a potential murder weapon? If you ask me, they were going to try to seek revenge for the kid who got stomped out and was shot several years prior, which I didn't commit for the record. I knew who did the shooting, but I am not a rat; I just had to take the loss and the blame, that's how it goes in the streets. I honestly know how it goes in the street; if someone wants to see you dead, the solution is to put a price (money to hire a killer) on that person's head. That person would be me, that's what the boy Cocky's father did who was this big-time drug dealer. This further frustrated me, street justice is what he wanted; I wanted to find a weapon and level the playing field by putting a shank in his messenger's neck. How would that end for me, a two-year sentence for assault would end in a lifetime in this cage I thought. There I was in the county jail being processed; I was sent to a place after processing called the Barge, which is a jail built on an old boat that sits on the Bronx River in New York, for Bronx and Queens County criminals or inmates. At Rikers Island, the local county jail is continuously overcrowded, and this was our destination. For now, this was a cold, old ship with nothing but miseries anchored to it.

My first night on this ship, I slept next to a Spanish dude. For some strange reason, the next day, the old man with the metal foot boot had switched places with that Spanish guy, which I surmise was to attack me in my sleep with that knife in his boot. Evil will place you in the shadow of death, but God put a stop to their plans at least for now. On that Sunday morning, I was transferred to Rikers Island and by this particular situation happening, it revealed to me once again that God was looking out for me and confirmed that this revenge being sought was no illusion, but a realistic threat. More importantly, I recognized that I would be able to hopefully make it out of this place alive and in one piece.

I was in the clear, at least that's what I thought for a moment until the next day arrived. I was in the hallway in Rikers Island, and I happened to make eye contact with a dude who went by the street name of Crazy Nave. This brother was shot up multiple times by another guy in my neighborhood by the name of Mr. White. Crazy Nave would wind up killing Mr. White, catching him slipping as it's called in the streets, by shooting him multiple times while he was with his daughter. He placed her in the back seat of a car, and in retaliation for Mr. White shooting him several years ago, attacked.

Honestly, my stomach started to turn; I wanted to deal with that brother, but I was more focused on my own situation of surviving and not stirring the pot, especially if I was just as guilty of my own dirt just like him. What was more important was going to be this bid I would have to do and my own drama. Moving along, I was handed over to the state of New York Department of Corrections and sent to my next facility, also known as Up North (Upstate New York). Man! That was the longest seven-hour bus ride I ever took in my life, shackled from my waist to my feet, having to utilize the restroom but not being able to.

The bus went from downstate Correctional Facility to Ulster County Correctional Facility to several other facilities before I would arrive at the Greene Correctional Facility. As soon as I arrived at this hoosegow, or in laymen's terms prison, I could see all the superficial truth of prison coming to full reality: from the guard tower to the razor-sharp barbed wire fences to the security cameras set to detect any signs of motion. I could only think about the horrifying, ironic and morbid thoughts of being raped in the shower or cut with an old, rusty knife across my face.

After we arrived, the next step was processing; this meant being deloused with a foreign chemical, shaved bareheaded and given state greens to wear. My number was 08r0585. We were dropped off after processing to be placed in a dorm of fifty other men: most of them, you guessed it, African American and Hispanic. I knew then that I wouldn't last long.

My first day walking to my dorm in prison, I walked past the old foes I hadn't seen in years. The reality was out of sight, out of mind. The guy by name of Jason, which I introduced several chapters ago, the one I had wrestled a knife from in the epic gang fight at the age of fifteen, and soon after learned that I had assaulted his cousin. Crossing paths with another individual like Jason only seemed to create more tension and reignite the animosity from years ago, but the only thing that mattered was doing my time and going home.

I was locked up in prison, crossing paths with sworn enemies. I was in a bad mental state, and this made it worse, the reality of being locked up for the first time as an adult. Now I had to watch my back and keep my nose clean at the same time. The mental stress was draining, and most days, a tremendous burden and thoughts of suicide crossed my mind a few times; I did my best to stay out of trouble. However, it was extremely difficult because the haters and my enemies were all around me, planning and plotting every step of the way against me.

I wanted to better myself while I had the time. I was able to take live, in-person courses from Marist college; I acquired over nine college credits. I also found myself going back to church and working under Pastor Prisk and under another inmate by the name Analdi Vargas, the only people that I could trust. I learned one important thing from that inmate; one day, while walking back to our dorm, I created a scenario that went like this: "If you met a girl who was a prostitute in her past life, would you forgive her past and marry her?"

He responded, "If the Lord changed her life, why not? We can all change."

To this day, I remember that conversation with him, and it is a constant reminder that people can and do change for the better, including me. However, I finally gave up due to the mental drain and depression. After months of lockdown, I was at a breaking point; I was tired of being in the same place, wearing the same clothes, and being told what to do. The bouts of racism in prison were so surreal; a corrections officer shared the first time he saw a "Nigga" or Black person at nine years old as a cigar hung out his 300lb month. Not long after that, I had one fight after another, and the last one was over the TV, which is a big no-no in prison. I know you're wondering why, after all this trouble and drama, I would get into a fight over something so frivolous. Simply put, because I wanted to watch the New York Knicks game, which was my superficial reason; but the real in-depth reason was that I was angry, lonely, bitter, and miserable.

LOST SOULS

What happened next was going to be my last time staying in that prison environment. The rest of the inmates happened to be Bloods who controlled the TV. When I unplugged the TV, I knew I was going to be kicked out of the compound, beaten up, cut, stabbed, or jumped. That night, the course of my incarceration would change, and my interactions with the other gang-affiliated inmates would change my prison journey for the worse. After unplugging the TV, as others watched the annoyingly superficial show called "Flava Flav," I ran and got my work gloves and I went to the bathroom where I know I could fight anyone who had a problem with me unplugging the TV. I knew how to fight, and I was tired of all those people at that time. The first guy (victim or idiot) I struck with my first punch; I cracked open his eye, and thereafter blood gushed everywhere. Even though people were taking showers, this fight was happening, at the same time, I was being jumped and hit by multiple inmates. Somehow the brawl ended, and I was physically, mentally, and once again emotionally drained. I tried to recover by going to sleep, which would prove to be a dreadful decision – two other inmates attacked me as I lay in my bed.

They caught me "slipping" (off guard) at a time when I was vulnerable. I had underwear and a t-shirt, no shoes or socks, and I was put into a headlock to the point where I couldn't breathe. The other dude punched me in my ribs and kidneys continuously, while the first guy pummeled my face; every punch was grueling. I could only think about not getting stabbed or cut on my face. However, God sent an angel in the form of my only friend and fellow inmate by the name of Clayton Brown, also known as L.I. because he was from Long Island. He was a good person, and at that time, this was why he came to my rescue. Basically, he was my guardian angel at that point. He helped me to get one dude off of me, and I went to work, unfortunately, on the other guy. And in retrospect, I beat the crap out of him as much as I could before the guards came to break up the fight.

At that moment, after all those things happened, over a state-owned TV, I felt as if I had failed again. The truth was I was angry at myself, frustrated, and upset once again at my current situation. I brought this onto myself because of my actions. I was immediately sent to the box, the S.H.U. (Special Housing Unit) as they call it to be politically correct, or as I like to say the hoosegow inside of the hoosegow. I didn't know it at the time, but this was going to be the place that would allow my mind to be exposed to the thoughts that were deep-rooted and to become more in touch with myself. The defining thoughts and epiphanies that would be discovered, which I would need to arrive at that specific junction in my life, happened here in this area of solitary confinement. I spent the next six months thinking over and over about all the things that had led me to this point.

However, as I said before, old habits die hard. I found myself in trouble even inside the solitary confinement. I will explain what happened in a moment. I was detained for twenty-three hours a day and allowed to shower once a week. For the most part, I found myself reading anything I could get my hands on just to keep my mind from running wild, everything from self-help books to novels. More importantly, I read the most important book that any Christian could read, or anyone who is lost could find, and that was the Holy Bible, the King James version, from front to back. I drew closer to the Lord and had numerous conversations with God about my life and what I was going to do after I finished my time. I exercised, wrote journals, letters, and learned how to do handstand push-ups and an array of workouts out of pure boredom.

Ironically, as I said before, all of this could not help me stay out of trouble and stay focused. I found myself in trouble even in the "Box" and was cut by a scalpel across my hand. Yes, you read that right! I was assaulted by another inmate with a surgical instrument called a scalpel. The reason behind the assault was because I didn't know how to control my emotions and my mouth once again. As a few of the inmates and I played a jail-made trivia game on the gate (cell bars), I became upset at this individual; it was over a game discrepancy. I insulted the guy who also happened to oversee the handling of all the food and making sure people got what they needed, such as toiletries; the porter which this position is called. In my anger, I told him to "suck my dick." In other words, the worst thing you can say to another man in prison, besides calling him a snitch.

The next day, he approached my cell in a fit of rage and began trying to reach through the bars to grab my arm out of my cell. Only after the altercation, which lasted for about a minute, did I realize he was trying to cut my wrist at my main arteries along my arm. If that happened, that would spell life-threating trouble and even death! Imagine if he had cut me correctly, I would have bled out in my cell, all due to the fact I lacked discipline. This was a harsh and cold reality to be learned. I realized that as I watched the blood pour from my finger, and I discovered that he had accomplished his goal of cutting me.

However, what we reap is what we sow, that same guy, who went by the alias D-Block, would not be able to return because he could not clear the mag or the metal detectors on his way to court from the S.H.U. He was relocated to another prison and given a new charge for concealing a weapon inside of his anus, or as they call it in prison his trunk. Yes, the same weapon that was used to cut me was found inside of his anus; prison was crazy and full of contraband such as this.

I was placed in solitary confinement with numerous other people, or as I like to say, other souls who were also incarcerated, serving time for various offenses. Let's start with the negative souls first; I was placed next to a real psychopathic thug by name of Nathaniel, who went by the alias "Nate the Great." He was a guy from Brownsville, Brooklyn, New York. This individual made me realize that some souls are just lost forever and will never be saved, will remain bitter, full of hate, and, unfortunately, remain behind bars forever. This guy loved to make all kinds of threats, such as he was going to shoot me, do all sorts of evil things to my family, all because he was angry at himself and his current situation. Honestly, he was almost forty and had been incarcerated for most of his adult life.

As time went on, our interactions lead him to threaten me with one of the worst possible threats besides physical harm. He threatened to "shit" me down, which meant, in layman's terms, that he was going to throw his feces into my cell, and God knows what kind of diseases he had.

On to the next lost soul, a young Black man who was also incarcerated with me, this guy called himself Jersey, and he was an okay guy until one day when I was on porter duty. Yes, I became the new porter since the old one who cut me was sent away to a new unit. This guy from Jersey tried to throw feces and urine on me as I walked past. That's right; he tried to throw his piss on the inmates and me next to his cell. Here's the real dangerous irony; he had HIV. So, it was a miracle that none of that bodily fluid landed in my face or my eyes because that could have been a bad situation.

The next soul went by the name "Bread Dollar." He represented the epitome of millennial gangsterism. This kid was a Spanish brother from uptown Manhattan, New York, and loved to play games, loved to talk, and he loved his tattoos which he had all over his arms and body. This guy seemed to have a head on his shoulders, and I ultimately knew that one day he could do something amazing with his life if he decided to change his course. He took his time to share with me some words of wisdom regarding prison life. As he was there when I went through that situation with the last porter, he told me, "Watch what you say out of your mouth." If this situation occurred in the population, I would have seriously been injured, and I could have lost my life.

The last soul was the most unique and profound of all the people I met in prison; the brother went by the name "China Don." That's right; his name was China. He was a high a general in the Blood street gang, I never found out what his real name was, but he was a short guy from Brooklyn, New York, who was one of those inmates who touched me to the soul. He spoke to the inner man in me; he inserted a new perspective into my mind.

China taught me many lessons about life, prison life, about women, business, and opportunities outside of the box, such as how to start my own company. I also learned how to treat women;

he truly enlightened me about how to approach females and what they were about, the importance of having integrity and loyalty. Unfortunately, I believe his sentence was ten to fifteen years.

The most bizarre thing that I had learned from this individual was that he was the gentleman who provided the guy who had cut me with the weapon. He apologized once he realized what happened to me. However, he schooled me to how life truly works in prison and what it would be like once I left Southport S.H.U. At this point, my isolation time was up, and it was time to return to the general population with all the other intimates, guilty or innocent.

SHAWSHANK REDEMPTION

After I left the S.H.U., unfortunately, I was then upgraded to a maximum-security prison due to my violent interaction with the Bloods gang members over the TV. I was happy to leave the prison inside the prison, but I was even more nervous when it was time to leave. I would be heading to the "big house" with hardened criminals. When I arrived outside of my next location, it looked like a scene straight out of the movie "Shawshank Redemption." I was shocked at how it was like something straight out of every prison movie I had ever watched, but worse because this wasn't a movie, it was my current reality. The prison which I was now going to be housed in had guards in watchtowers with guns, barbed wire electric fences, and a wall. The place looked like Fort Knox. It was mind-boggling to contemplate what to expect behind these twenty-foot walls. Most of the prisoners would be locked away there for ten years to life. Entering this environment with the mindset of me-against-the-world is the only way I would be able to survive; my mind started to go crazy. I would learn about inmates who were incarcerated for various crimes ranging from sexual assault, robbery, to even murder.

In my first week at Wende Correctional Facility, I met a brother by the name of Darnell who was from upstate New York, Buffalo, and was locked up for a serious sexual offense. He became a close comrade. His personality reminded me of George from the book *Of Mice and Men*. He was six feet, two inches and husky, a real gentle giant, he showed me around and how everything operated. For example, "Never look in another inmate's house (cell); this can cause fights or problems." I was culture-shocked at all the rules of this micro-society.

I also met another brother from upstate New York, who went by the name "So What." That's right; his name was "So What." I can't make this stuff up, and that's what I called him. This brother had the potential to play at least D2 or D1 basketball. He was that good in the yard; however, he was serving a fifteen- year sentence at the age of twenty-five.

During my stay at Wende Correctional Facility, I saw people get into gang fights, stabbings, and I found myself at one point in time holding a plastic knife made from raw materials to protect myself. One day, in the yard, while talking to other inmates, without paying any mind to my proper speaking or my decent grasp of English grammar, I rambled. However, after having a conversation or two with those fellow inmates, my comrade, Darnell, informed me that I should not be using such elaborate words because people may become offended by my good grammar and consider it an insult, as if I was better than them.

This was one of the main reasons, amongst the violence and lack of freedom, that made me realize this place was not for me and I was out of place. In fact, in the wrong place, humans aren't meant to be put in cages, neither are animals, it's inhumane, there are truly other ways to rehabilitate; honestly, the prison industrial complex isn't about making offenders better. That incident has been cemented in my memory, even up until this day, to remind me that I could never be in such a place where my intelligence needed to be downplayed or watered down for the sake of my survival.

My time at Wende Correctional Facility was enough to realize that this was not where I wanted to be for the rest of my life. My release date, or as they say in prison, "until the wake up," was several months away. Once again, I learned the hard way about being very mindful of what I say to others.

One Sunday morning, while on the gate leaning against the cell bars, there was a conversation going on involving several inmates, including myself. One inmate raved about how he didn't believe in God or Jesus, and I stated some facts of my own belief. As the cliché states – never talk about sex, religion or politics in public, or this instance, prison. The dude shouted out something slanderous regarding Christianity and I responded with a fervent tone to the defense of my belief.

What transpired next was something out of a nightmare. An individual once again confronted me with a weapon in hand in the form of a scalpel, and this individual stood in front of me with the bars removed; in other words, we were face-to-face. He yelled, "Say something else about me being crazy again…" We locked gazes, eye to eye, and I could see the anger and animosity in his soul!

At that moment, my friend Darnell, another guardian angel, hopped in between this deranged inmate and me. Forevermore, that situation, as well as all the others, always sticks in my mind and reminds me that had I made the wrong choice to fight back. I could have wound up spending more time in prison, more so the lesson to learn was to be mindful of what I say to others, everyone is entitled to their own opinions even if they are ludicrous. The situation was quickly de-escalated.

Meanwhile, as all of this transpired, the prison guard just stood at the end of the hall, watching the whole situation. It ended with me humbly apologizing to the inmate and going to church that Sunday morning with brother Darnell. The irony of that situation was that I only had ninety days until my wake-up call to go home. I had already blown my chances for an early release date by fighting. In hindsight, as this inmate stood in front of me, with a weapon in hand, all I could think about was my mother and my release date to go home and that this was the only thing that mattered. That kept me from going after this dude even though he could have seriously hurt me by cutting me with that surgical weapon.

The moral to this experience of having your freedom taken away for the umpteenth time was that when you do not listen to your parents or take heed to the wisdom being given, you find yourself here. Taking heed to those who have lived before you and experienced similar situations is vital in life, you will continuously find yourself in heartache, loneliness, bitterness, anger, self-hatred, and regret as a result of not listening to the wisdom of others. It is imperative that as a young man(person) in this society we adhere to instructions from those who have lived before us, trust me, it will save you lots of time and headaches from regret.

WAKE-UP CALL TO GO HOME

After serving several years of my life in and out of state custody, confinement, and lastly, the penitentiary, I was released from prison in January 2010. I was released back into society and wasn't prepared to face the social, financial, and economic realities of being a Black man on parole in America, let alone New York City.

I was released from prison and taken to a bus station with my belongings inside a prison laundry bag, $85 in cash, and a Grey Hound bus ticket back to New York City from upstate New York. Having been denied my freedom, due to the legality and guilty

plea that I reluctantly accepted; I was anxious. Once again, I was put in a new situation. Thankfully, I acquired some college credits and landscaping skills while incarcerated. These still wouldn't be enough tools to operate in today's cronyism, nepotism, and experience-driven society. However, I was blessed with something even better, a support system in my family and friends.

After reluctantly returning to my old neighborhood in Queens, New York, I remember taking the longest shower I could and having the best dinner with my mother, father, and sister I could ever have. The tears of joy rolled down my face; the feeling of being free and being able to open my refrigerator at 2:00 a.m. is difficult to describe. You often take things for granted on the outside, such as being able to nibble on snacks, leftovers, and to drink juice from the container and spend time with the ones you love. All of these things never felt so good.

Thereafter, reality set in quickly. I would have to report to my parole officer, who went by the name of Mr. Pinnock. I will never forget this man's name. Mr. Pinnock was a Black, West Indian, short man, a complete asshole jaded by years of being a bureaucrat without any recognition for his hard work, and he treated me no differently than if I was just another number, which I was, just above the degree of scum or gum on the bottom of your shoe.

To make matters worse, along with his attitude of pure disgust, was the fact that his office was located in the wrong neighborhood. It felt like going behind enemy lines to negotiate with someone who controlled your destiny and freedom. His office was located right on Jamaica Avenue, which was one of the most populated shopping areas in the whole of South and North Queens between Hollis Avenue and South Jamaica, Queens. Every time I visited my parole officer, it felt like a head rush and a roller coaster ride gut feeling at the same time. I was anxious and nauseous. I had to see this man to remain free, but ironically to stay out of the crosshairs of clear and present danger, which always seemed to lurk nearby. Other inmates from prison I would frequently encounter made matters worse; the tension was always thick in the lobby of the parole office.

During the first interview with my parole officer, I explained to him my upbringing, my shortcomings, and my willingness to change, but this explanation fell on deaf ears. None the less, I told him a similar scenario I had faced before of almost being killed by a Judas of a friend. His response was, "If someone tries to shoot you or do harm to you, you must do your best to maneuver out of the situation and call the police."

The man was dead serious about his advice; he was basically telling me that I had no options when it came to the issues of potential violence in a community where this was the culture. I soon realized the horrible truth; my parole officers' job was to put me back behind bars and to help increase the recidivism rate. Therefore, it was going to be my job to stay free and, more importantly, to stay alive and ultra-productive at the same time. Elevation is key to survival in this world via education and street smarts (ghetto vigilance), coupled with faith.

Not only was I on parole, but I was now also on trial and guilty in the court of public opinion. I would be denied many opportunities and given no benefit of the doubt. This made it extremely hard readjusting back to society, even with my peers and my family, living in their home for the first time in years. In retrospect, it was the best place for me to be at the time. However, not long after I moved back home, I got into a big fight with my younger sister, Lindsay, it was a very bad physical fight, and as a result, she called the police that night in anger and spitefulness. Like a suspense thriller, the police left my parents' home after taking my sister's report, along with my mother's plea to my sister not to press charges (that would mean back to prison). To make matters worse, guess who walked up to do a house check at that very moment? I was horrified to see my parole officer, Mr. Evil Pinnock, so as he saw the police leaving, he smiled a cynical smile and stated, "Well, well, well, what is going on here?" I knew then and there I was going to be arrested again for violation of parole due to police contact.

My sister enthusiastically explained the situation in full detail, which ended with her stating the obvious, "I don't want him here!" My parole officer concluded that I would have to leave my parents' house or go back to jail. This news was a devastating blow to my progress; where was I going to go? Unfortunately, that situation forced me to leave my mother's house for good at twenty-one years old with no source of income, savings, or place to live.

In retrospect, that was the best thing that could have happened to me at that time, because if I had not been forced to leave my mother's house, in my old neighborhood, I probably would have wound up dead in a matter of weeks once the word got out that I was home from prison.

So, I was provided an opportunity to stay at my Aunt Carol's house, which fortunately I moved into once I left my mother's house. All other family members who had homes rejected my request to stay with them, including my cousin Petra whom my parents allowed to live rent-free for years. This hurt me very much to realize that the people I thought were supposed to help me, or at least give me a chance, turned their backs on me. This was a harsh reality check to know that family and friends did not want to be around someone who they felt was a criminal. The stares and whispers were very challenging to deal with, but I had no choice but to prove to myself that I could and would do better. My circumstance reminded me of the prejudice that I would continue to face for the rest of my life post-incarceration.

As I found myself living with my aunt and cousins, this was not a new experience for me, having just left the hoosegow full of strangers. As for my Aunt Carol, who indeed is a character and a unique person, we got along well. She was a typical, single, African American woman working the graveyard shift while maintaining as a city worker. She managed to raise two kids on her own since my uncle was shot and killed in the streets. My aunt was kind enough to also raise my two cousins from my Uncle Stanley. My older cousin, who has lived with my aunt since he was sixteen and never really had a father figure in his life, never seemed to find the drive to aspire to leave my aunt's house and do better. My cousin, Stanley, was a bit of an insecure and shallow guy, and all he did was collect sneakers and surf the Internet. He allowed me to see that it is dangerous not to have a vision or goals and how compliancy is toxic. For example, I noticed my cousin working on his beat machine, the beats sounded amazing! So, I stated, "Bro, if you stay focused on this, one day you can be a producer and become a millionaire."

He looked at me in pure disbelief and shock and stated, "No, I'm not!" This interaction reminded me that I didn't want to become complacent and afraid of success or reaching my full potential. I couldn't surround myself with this kind of mentality, it would be contagious; this created more motivation to leave as soon as possible. He was in his own mental prison entrapped by his own visual limitations, as are so many people in the inner cities of America and around the world.

My little cousin seemed to follow the footsteps of my older cousin, which was better than following mine or his older brother Elijah's path. I hit the ground walking, in search of employment, especially since my parole officer offered no resources. I mean, how does the

American society expect people who have been released from prison to become productive and to remain crime-free if no one wants to hire you because of your blemish(s) on your record? This cycle only forces people back into a life of crime, or addiction which leads to crime to fuel the addiction. Learning through my own research, I realized the system post-incarceration is designed for the failure of all those who have been spit out of the prison industrial machine back into society in order to be recycled right back in. After weeks of "No's" by potential employers due to my background, on a more positive note, I finally found myself a job working at the biggest Foot Locker in New York City, or the world for that matter. I started working at Foot Locker on West 34th Street, in Manhattan, New York, across the street from the largest Macy's in the world, in March 2010. Thanks to a guy by the name of Juan Melendez, who was the store manager, I was given a chance although I had a record.

At one point, I was one of the top sellers in the store. I was given an opportunity, although I had made numerous mistakes in the past. I learned the ins and outs of the American corporate system. I was hired to work, but at the same time, the company received a corporate tax incentive to hire people with criminal records. So, after securing employment, it was a relief, but this was only the first step of my journey.

When I came home from prison, systematically, I was supposed to succumb to the pressure of my environment and revert to crime.

Thanks to my family and friends, I was able to transcend the odds and be productive.

TWO WOMEN

I was twenty-one years old, starting a new life after incarceration, after living as a juvenile who was in and out of jail and in and out of trouble. I was faced with many peer pressures after I came back home. I still had to deal with the pressure from my old cronies who smoked weed and were involved with street dealings. The stigma of a felon is like having lesions on you toward the society at large, but in the neighborhood, it is an absurd rite of passage or badge of honor.

While avoiding trouble in my neighborhood, I was kicked out of my mother's house, as I said before, due to a fight with me and my sister. Moving forward, after living with my aunt for almost a year and having to deal with my cousins eating all my food, living like sardines, and always getting on my nerves, I learned quickly that I didn't like living there. I needed to move away into my comfort zone, or better yet, stand on my own two feet as a young man.

How was I going to do that? Rent was so expensive in New York, and I didn't know where to start being a first-time renter and on my own. On the other hand, on a personal, masculine note, I was truly in touch with my heterosexuality, and my hormones had been brewing like a hot can of soda that had been shaken before being opened. In other words, I was horny, full of sexual tension, anger, and many other emotions.

So, I started dating and trying to hump anything and everything that moved female wise. During this phase of extreme random promiscuity, I found myself a young lady whom I met on the train at the Hoyt and Schermerhorn station in downtown Brooklyn while coming from seeing my new parole officer. Her name was Tonya Garvey. She looked like a typical hood chick; you know the type, fly girl with fresh Kickz (sneakers), Asian-done nails, tight jeans, and natural hair. I was enthralled, or better yet, infatuated by this female and her style. Tonya was hot at the time, I must add. As time went on and the months passed, I found myself hanging out with this young lady more and more. As we spent more time together, I made one of the poorest decisions a man could make due to lack of discipline. I wound up getting her pregnant. I purchased the morning-after pill and tried to persuade her to have an abortion. She had a different opinion and refused to terminate her pregnancy.

As she was getting ready to give birth we always argued, and one day it got to the point where she became violent. As I drove down the street, she grabbed the steering wheel of the car and tried to kill us; we had a physical fight, unfortunately. This led to me thinking about my future, which in hindsight, I was putting the carriage before the horse. I had to tell this young lady the truth: I wouldn't be able to help raise this child due to the dangers lurking from my past. I had no intention of raising a baby in New York City, nor did I have the means. I didn't want to become a super hourly-wage worker at a dead-end job and a super dad on weekends in the hood. I desired to leave and return to school so I could have a valid career in order to provide for my son.

Moving forward, she gave birth several weeks later to a boy. We named my son Joseph Harvey and unfortunately, I was not ready. I was so immature that I wasn't even there to see him born on February 26th, 2011, which was almost one year after I was released from the hoosegow.

The thing that made this situation even worse was the fact that not only was I transitioning from my past situation of being incarcerated and trying to hold down a J.O.B. – which stands for being just over broke – I had no one to blame but myself for my baby woes. Also, my mother did warn me about sleeping around. So here I was once again facing a new, unique life situation, a young African American man with a record, a father, flunked out of high school, a G.E.D. holder, and most importantly, no college education or trade to my name.

As a man of faith, I had come to learn and realize that God is in control of everything. Jesus had a plan for my life at this point, and my son was just a part of the plan. Joseph would become the fuel that I needed emotionally, physically, and mentally to jumpstart my ambition and attack life head-on. I had to decide if I was going to continue to be a little boy or grow into a man of responsibility and distinction; no doubt there would be peaks and valleys of learning experiences ahead.

Although on parole, I still found myself having to deal with going to anger management classes because I needed help managing my emotions, also a drug program since I was a chronic smoker of marijuana, and a few other mandatory release programs. During this time of being a new father, working a full-time job, living with three other people, and not having any major plans for the foreseeable future, I was depressed, to be honest. However, I would find myself waiting for a date in Times Square, right in front of the Deaune Reade drug store across from the police station, in the center of 42nd Street. The date would wind up standing me up, I didn't know it at the time as I was ignorant of many things, but I would meet a young lady by the name of Yaunita Anderson from Houston, Texas.

I had to look twice. The second look coming from a double take, this sister had on red tights with polka dot underwear. I remember it like it was yesterday. She had one of the largest gluteus maximus I had ever seen in my life, a southern swag as well and the accent. I followed her into the store like the real thirsty (longing) guy that I was because I was desperate for an opportunity to meet somebody new and someone who appealed to me, finally. Our interaction was short and brief. We exchanged numbers and I discovered she was in town because she was here for an Eastern Star conference, and she so happened to drive up to New York for the day with her fellow fraternity members. It was honestly my first time meeting a girl from Texas.

From then on, we kept in touch day and night, and we decided to create a long-distance friendship. Within the next several months, I found an apartment for both of us to stay in, located in Flatbush, Brooklyn, New York. I didn't know it at the time but living in the heart of Flatbush would turn out to be a horrific idea. Willingly, I moved out of my aunt's house into that apartment with a girl I was getting to know.

I would find myself in a full-blown relationship living with this woman from Texas and her friend named Brooke. Well, with this new life of playing house, as the old folks call it, I still had to stand on my feet and provide my end of the rent. Later in life, I learned that you aren't a man until your name is on the lease or mortgage. I would also get to see my son on the weekends; this was all a new experience for me. Eventually, the mother of my son would force me back into court for an expected payday in the form of more child support.

I worked at Foot Locker for as long as I could, almost two years, and it was my first full-time corporate job ever. However, my position in the corporation would not sustain for much longer due to my old ways resurfacing in my attitude and also my lack of understanding of corporate changes. What I didn't learn and understand was that in corporate America, or when working for someone else, things change all the time to help the bottom line of the corporation. In other words, to bring in more profit for the company, not you as the slave; sorry, I meant employee.

I found myself not being able to adapt quickly and smoothly to the new system of how sales and products were delivered, which, in turn, affected my paycheck as a commissioned worker. My checks began to dwindle, and I started to become more and more anxious because the bills began to become more and more of a giant in my shadow every payday. Rent, child support, savings, and other expenses were overwhelming; I had more month than check left most times.

One day I got so frustrated as I waited for another co-worker to give me a product as the customer waited and waited until they left – due to the new corporate change. My tolerance was at the all-time low, my patience was null and void. I lost my cool and went on a tirade in a fit of rage. It became so bad that I had to be escorted off the premises and found myself waiting outside of the job to address the fellow employees I felt were the cause of my demise.

I would soon learn in retrospect that the only person that caused my demise was me; failure to asses, adapt, and act accordingly cost me my livelihood. So now, at this point, not only was my son in need of items and food, but also now I was unemployed and providing for myself and my girlfriend would become a major struggle. So, I was moving in the right direction with parole and my new place; however, I just couldn't seem to get my emotions right, as I tried to move forward. I had trouble adjusting to being on my own and dealing with the realities of life after prison.

Furthermore, this was all a new experience for me as I have never lived with so many people besides family and other inmates. The life education would never stop; life is like being in a constant classroom learning lesson after lesson, some hard and some easy, but constantly learning.

I learned many things about myself from that relationship; it came with many ups and downs, arguments, fights, and good times. One of the benefits was that I had several opportunities to travel to Texas during the two years I dated this woman. I traveled back and forth to Houston, Texas, several times that year in 2012, and when I went down south for the first time, what I saw was priceless. I saw African American unity and family appreciation like I had never seen in my life. On top of that, the weather was immaculate even during the wintertime compared to New York City.

I fell in love with the southern hospitality, I had many great initial experiences, my first time having a Caucasian man hold the door open for me in kindness and saying, "Howdy." I turned back afterwards in shock; I was so ignorant of the southern culture I thought it was a prelude to being hung or a setup.

I also had my first experience ever attending a gun show. As I walked past the vast number of guns on display, a White woman walked toward me, and her shirt displayed a picture of President Obama and a lion. The shirt stated, "African Lion, Lying African." I stared at the shirt in such disbelief and such culture, to point Yuanita had to raise her voice and yank my arm to get me out of the racial trance.

Every time I went to Texas, it felt like I was on vacation, honestly; I mean from the food portion sizes, and from the way people interacted with each other, it made me realize that I needed to move there. I remembered my old friend and mentor, Mr. Shawn Farnum, telling me, "The only thing you need is a change of geographical location to create a fresh start for yourself."

THE GREAT MOVE

So, for nearly two years, I lived in Flatbush, Brooklyn. During that time, I struggled with becoming a new father, being in a new relationship with an older woman, and being fired from my full-time job at Foot Locker to find myself. Then I decided to create my own business for the first time.

When I realized that I was unemployed, I immediately filed for unemployment insurance, and thank God, I qualified. The unemployment insurance was enough to pay my portion of the rent and stay afloat until I found another job. So, I found myself thinking about all the possible solutions. One solution that came to mind was an instance when my dad, also known as Brother Will, had told me about a way he was making money on the side. For a time, I owned a contractual salvage company, but due to lack of experience and education, it failed. Let me share the story.

My father worked for a medical supply corporation attached to Rikers Island where they threw away massive amounts of metal, and he would just put it in the dumpster outside his job for many years. All this time, he would come back to work the next day to find the dumpster empty. One day, my father saw a familiar homeless man who happened to be taking stuff out of the dumpster. My father humbly asked the gentleman, "Sir, what do you do with this metal you take out of the dumpster?"

The homeless man replied, "Brother Will, since you have always been so kind to me and allowed me to take out of your dumpster all these years, I will tell you what I do, or as I call it, I will give you the hidden gem."

Well, the hidden gem was that anyone could sell scrap metal for a profit. The homeless man would take the metal out of the dumpster and transport it to scrap brokers or scrap yards and be paid a pretty penny by the pound for this recycled metal. This was a whole industry which generated billions of dollars a year, and my father would share this hidden gem with me

So, Yaunita and I put together a plan; and for the record, she sponsored the venture to do scrap metal and salvaging full time. We purchased our first van for seven hundred dollars, which, of course, broke down in two weeks. However, I was able to make three times what the van was worth in those two weeks, working for myself. I had to scrap it for about seven hundred bucks once it broke down. I took the proceeds and purchased a newer van thereafter in order to continue the business. After that, I was able to create a sustainable scrap metal and salvage business; this enterprise only enlightened and enticed me.

I found myself earning several hundred dollars a day. Being on my own was a surreal experience. It was very daunting at first. I soon realized that being an entrepreneur was not only a great experience, which not only required a lot of responsibility, but also, this would be my ultimate goal in the future.

I traveled like never before in my life post parole. Since I made my schedule as an entrepreneur during this time, I was able to go back to Jamaica for the first time since an adolescent. This was my mother's home country; it felt good to tap into my roots. I also went to the Dominican Republic, Punta Cana & Santa Domingo, Miami's South Beach, New Orleans, Louisiana, and Texas several times in one year. All of this was a taste of the good life after prison and all of my ups and downs.

You may be wondering how I could leave the country while on parole. I had reached a significant milestone in order to travel; I had successfully completed parole with the help of my new parole officer Ms. Johnson. I was also able to receive a certificate of relief from disabilities, which acts as a form of restoration regarding basic civil rights, such as my right to vote, obtain specific jobs, and, most importantly, reclaim my liberty to pursue happiness (success). However, I would never be able to bear arms in order to protect myself and my family or get a decent municipal job, such as a firefighter, as we will see in the next couple of chapters.

However, this euphoric feeling, which came with my transitional success, would, unfortunately, be short-lived. I was struck by a car on Flatbush Ave in Brooklyn while riding my bike to get a haircut on Friday the 13th, April 2012. I was hit on my right side of my body on my knee.

I was rushed to the hospital and treated. I was bedridden for several weeks and attended physical therapy three times a week for several months. I can only once again thank God that I only suffered a torn meniscus, partially torn ACL, a pinched nerve, and a bulging disk. I could have been hit by a bigger vehicle or even a bus for that matter; I was once again blessed to have avoided death.

Thereafter, my time living in Brooklyn would abruptly end. I didn't realize that although I had moved out of my old neighborhood, I didn't move far enough. In fact, I went from one inner-city neighborhood to a worse one located in Flatbush, Brooklyn, of all places. I moved to East 26th between Albemarle and Tilden, off Nostrand Avenue. If you are from Brooklyn, you know this is a terrible area. I made the mistake of going back to my old neighborhood, and while at a red light, I made eye contact with a kid named Nokia, who is now serving life for killing another guy from the neighborhood over a dispute, a local Bloods gang member named Trillip.

That was it; my cover was blown. I found myself in an unfortunate situation one evening while riding my bike down Nostrand Avenue, and someone shouted out my government name, Jon Marc. To my surprise, it was two older gentlemen from my old neighborhood in Queens. To be exact, it was Mikey, aka "Ike stacks," and an ugly dread named Zah (a low life drug dealer). I spoke to them out of respect and to give the art of "Never let them see you sweat," I played it cool and then removed myself out of their presence as soon as I could. At that moment in time, I knew that they were on to me and knew where I now lived. It also didn't help that I had a blond Mohawk at the time, it was a phase, a true expression of freedom, yet a loud hairstyle.

Several weeks later, one Saturday night, I happened to be in my kitchen after walking my girlfriend's dog and coming in from smoking some weed on the stoop. Then, in several minutes, I overheard a very loud group of people and very intense but deep conversation between my neighbor and some other guys. I went to my window out of pure curiosity and turned off the lights. As I did, I heard strangers stressing the fact that I had been incarcerated, and one guy stating, "Yeah, he knows we are looking for him."

My neighbor replied, "I never really liked the dude. I knew something about him wasn't right. He and his girl got into an argument the other day."

I was being thrown under the bus, and quickly.

He also stated to the strange men, "Sometimes he has problems getting into his door, his lock jams."

One stranger replied, "We're going to get him tomorrow. Don't say anything. We don't want him to know you are involved."

From that moment, I began to revert to my street-smarts once again and thought about my next move. Although I had purchased a .380 Taurus pistol for my girlfriend while in Texas, who was legally allowed to carry it, ironically, she had it confiscated several weeks prior at the airport. In my fit of anger, I ran to the room to grab that gun and then to head outside to face my foes the ignorant street way. Thank God the gun wasn't there.

I had survived being beaten up, juvenile detention, prison, parole, being nearly cut with machetes, attacked with a knife, cut, and now I was going to have to survive being shot and possibly killed by vengeful foes who had the scoop from my Judas-like neighbors. The irony of the whole situation was I never did anything wrong to my neighbors. In fact, in retrospect, I asked one of the guys one day to buy weed for me and he scammed me out of my five dollars change. Never trust street dudes or gangbangers, guys who drink and smoke their lives away on the block; they prove to be jealous and envious plotters in the end. The crab in a barrel mentality is a major epidemic in the African American community; whether it is inherited via slavery or obtained through the 21st-century experience, it is detrimental.

That Saturday, before overhearing the intricate plot to end my life, I had just called my dad to ask him if he needed help with cleaning the church, which he did part-time. Before that, as I said earlier, I had smoked a joint and walked the dog. As I sat outside and observed the street, my instincts told me to go into the house, and I did.

Well, the plot was in play, and I now had the drop on these fools, this led me to act. I called friends and family, mainly my mother, for needed advice. I felt like my world was falling apart again for the millionth time. 'How could this happen again?' I thought. I just started a business. I was traveling and working hard to stay out of jail. As this plot was transpiring, my girlfriend and I were at odds, my supplemental unemployment income was coming to an end, I just finished real-estate school, I had just renewed my apartment lease, and more importantly, my son was just born. It meant that I would have to make a tough choice, stay, and defend my pride and life, which came with the risk of death, or leave and live to concur another day.

I decided to pack up my entire life in that one night; it helped because my girlfriend had gone to Texas that week. My girlfriend's friend/roommate Brooke moved back to Texas strangely several weeks before. Was it because she was sleeping with the neighbors and caught wind of the plot? I will never know. So, I packed up an entire apartment on my own.

The next day, I took the essentials and my girlfriends' dog with me, leaving the boxes, and I stayed with my parents for a few days. I had to explain my story several times to numerous friends and family members in order for them to understand. It felt like I was living out a movie, several of my family members exclaimed. The whole week I did nothing but plan my next move because certainly, my time was up in New York City or maybe "on this side of eternity," as my father loves to say.

I urged my mother and father to assist me in buying a plane ticket to Houston, Texas, and that's what I did. Later that week, with the help of my cousin, Elijah, and my brother, Ruben, for protection, I rented a U-Haul van and went back to my old apartment in Flatbush, Brooklyn, to grab the remainder of my clothes, personal items and my girlfriend's dog. As I pulled up to my apartment, a guy in a hoodie, with an orange duffle bag, took off running from the street corner in front of my house. That was confirmation: it was time to go. However, the plot to kill me was real because he was waiting and lurking in order to see his task completed- my death.

As I packed the U-Haul rental van, my "Judas" neighbor came out of his apartment in thespian astonishment to inquire about why I was leaving my apartment. I was wearing a Navy t-shirt and told him, "I'm going to the Navy."

Unbeknown to him, I knew about the intricate plot to do me in which he was conspicuously a part of willingly. The hatred brewed inside me as he stood in front of me. I just wanted to kill him for his blatant and unwarranted betrayal; he reminded me as I stood there eyeing him that there is no loyalty in the streets. I had to use restraint not to knock this dude out, but just like that last incident in prison, sometimes you must swallow your pride to survive and live literally to fight another day.

I placed my things in storage, moved out of Brooklyn, and found myself on a plane that week to Houston, Texas. At this point, again, I had to be separated from my immediate family, my son, and yet again, finding myself isolated in a different part of the country, having to start over emotionally, socially, and financially for the third time.

DEEP IN THE HEART OF THE SOUTH

My unemployment was running out at this point, so was the patience of my girlfriend, and she and I were at the end of our relationship. When I arrived in Houston, Texas, I felt like a chicken with its head cut off, socially and financially. I was depressed, angry, unstable, and uncomfortable yet again. I didn't have the ability to realize it then, but I needed to feel those feelings of discomfort and fear to be where I am now. I would have to find the strength and wherewithal to uplift myself out of depression through positive self-coaching, daily introspection, and understanding that I needed to utilize my indignation as a driving force toward blind success.

I chose to use the uncomfortable feeling to move toward consistency and ultimately toward success, although truthfully, I didn't know what it looked like at the time.

To add to my woes, I didn't have a car either; I technically didn't have my own place, food, or a job more importantly. I relied on the sole person who had helped me so many times before, my ex-girlfriend, Yaunita, and my only significant line of support here in Texas at the time. She did her best to show her true kindness and southern hospitality; she showed me around.

The choice to move was broken down into two options, either stay in New York and return to prison after killing someone in self-defense or be killed (like so many of my comrades before me). Both those options were dead ends, and so I chose neither. Instead I chose life and the opportunity to become successful, although this would be sacrificing everything I knew.

Under these unfortunate circumstances life seemed to be getting worse by the minute. Here I was facing these new uphill battles; I was trying to figure out who I was as a man, who I wanted to become, how to be responsible, and to stand on my own two feet. I hit the ground running once I had the opportunity to. Every day for two months, my friend and now ex-girlfriend, Yaunita, and I ritually dropped her mother off at work and drove around to different companies so I could apply for jobs. I applied to over ten jobs, Walmart, Subway, Office Depot, etc. They all said no because I had a criminal record. However, I had served my time in prison, successfully completed parole, received my certificate of relief from disabilities, which is a law under Article 23 – A of the NYC Correction Law. I was still denied employment by these so-called "jobs," my hands were tied, and my brain was fried from the constant denial.

I learned the hard lesson about bureaucratic policies and state laws during this initial job search. I learned that every state has its own laws and does not have to recognize the laws of another state, including my written legal proof of rehabilitation (in turn, legally each state is its own country/ jurisdiction), what a hard lesson.

More importantly, I was running out of unemployment benefits, and making matters worse, I am a Black man, with only a GED, no real work experience, a father unable to provide, and a felon in the deep south. I thought to myself out loud after a day's worth of job searching I couldn't even get a job as a janitor cleaning the toilet for one company that had nothing but Mexican workers.

I was feeling depressed, low and defeated at a few points, away from family, my son, which added to my frustration stemming from being stalked like prey by my foes in NYC. Things only got worse, and eventually, my ex-girlfriend and her mother, Ms. Flanderson, became frustrated and tired of my presence in their home. I am truly grateful for the opportunity I was given. The truth is people lose respect for you after a while and this can lead to resentment. As I reflect, I would feel the same kind of way if there was a boy living in my house rent free and not doing anything with his life. I say boy because I wasn't a man yet; a man takes care of his family and makes a living. I wasn't there yet, but Yaunita would try to help me get on the right track one last time before she could leave in good conscious. Point being, I was totally out of options and grace. I had one more check from my unemployment for several hundred dollars.

Yaunita, being smart and resourceful, decided to challenge me with the thought of going back to school in order to further my education. I was honestly apprehensive due to my educational failure in the past, but this was the light bulb moment I had been waiting for, or, better yet, the opportunity I should have taken and completed several years prior. However, this is how life works. So, I brainstormed and researched my available options, which were Houston Community College, Texas Southern University, or a school outside of Houston called Prairie View A&M University. The options dropped down to PVAMU.

Prior to this new enrollment strategy, I had failed out of community college a few times due to math. The school was far away from city life, which also meant far from trouble, at least that was the idea once again. I went to this new school with Yaunita, would be there to help me through the whole process by driving back and forth an hour each way to the school many days. I finally completed the application process thank God, which required my last several hundred dollars with a $150 medical checkup, a $60 application fee, and a few other requirements such as my SAT scores, which I had reluctantly taken several years before. Now the scores and the last check would come in handy, hopefully setting me up for success.

I never thought I would pursue college ever again after failing out several times back in New York due to poor grades and tuition issues. While applying to go back to school, I truly realized that it was indeed time to be my own person and to make something out of myself. I submitted my documents to the admissions office to a little lady named Ms. Wallace, who would, unfortunately, pass away a few months before I graduated. However, good news would come in the form of a letter from Prairie View A&M University, that I was accepted on conditional acceptance and due to start in January 2013, the spring semester.

I was excited to be granted the opportunity to attend the second oldest University in Texas and the oldest Black university in Texas. However, I still was very nervous because I was a bit timid and insecure about being back in school at an older age with younger students.

One Sunday afternoon, I was dropped off by Yuanita with my suitcase and my newfound ambition to graduate from college, finally. Here I was once again starting a fresh chapter in my life after prison and now back in college. I would later discover distant relatives who worked at the school and attended PVAMU.

I started as a nursing major and quickly decided that I wanted to become a physical education teacher, which was my original goal. I figured this was the only class I enjoyed as a kid in school and that

I loved exercising, staying active, and basketball, so why not go to school for it?

The mental euphoria would be short-lived, and life would once again deal me a sobering blow in the form of student housing. Before I came to school, I had done all the possible calculations, or that was what I thought. Well, according to student housing, I still needed to put forth a down payment on my house, which cost about $500. As I sat in the student housing office explaining my story to several staff members, a manager by the name of Mr. Davis reached into his wallet and gave me all his money. It was exactly $300, which was enough to allow me to move in. I was in total shock and disbelief that a stranger would be so generous and incredibly gracious in helping me!

THE FIREHOUSE

T he next three years would be full of ups and downs, good times, and bad times. I made it onto the dean's list for excellent grades; I was also hauled into the student code of conduct office for several disputes and required to take anger management, yet again.

I found myself with a lot of idle time, and therefore, I volunteered around campus. One day I discovered a Volunteer Fire Department in the area. My first encounter was over the phone with the safety officer, whom I later discovered was Captain Rodney; I was told I couldn't volunteer. As he put it, "Families in their times of loss, fellow firefighters and police officers wouldn't be comfortable knowing someone with a record was around on the fire ground."

I didn't take no for an answer; I decided to go up to the station and talk to someone. I remember riding up on my bike, to the building called the Al Bowdre Fire Station.

The first person I saw and spoke to was an older man named Al Bowdre. I explained to him my past and my aspirations to volunteer in order to make social amends and give back to the community. He told me, "Just keep coming by."

I heeded his advice, and for nearly four years throughout college, I served and even received a Rookie of the Year award for serving the community.

I also found a job working in the school gym for a coach by the name of Lee Gillian or Coach G, who was an old school "Kappa" from Chicago. He provided me the opportunity to work in a relaxed and fun environment.

During my first month of school, I got into a fight with a student over something simple, you guessed it, a basketball. I was playing with too much New York edge, and he decided to push me. He crossed the line putting his hands on me, and not knowing me and all the tension I had pent up inside, we got into a fight, and I let out all of my frustration on this guy. It turned into a big deal, but the point is Coach G made sure I didn't get into any trouble with the campus police or the student code of conduct.

That incident was perhaps one that could have landed me out of school before I had even gotten started. I tried my best to move forward and keep my nose clean. Coach G went on to not only be my boss but also, most importantly, he became my mentor. He was an example I needed to continue to discover my identity and purpose.

One day he sat me down in his office and explained to me that he wanted to get me from here, working in the gym, to graduation. He pointed to his wall of students who had matriculated. That day Coach G also explained to me a concept that has resonated with me ever since. He said, "J," which he affectionately referred to me as, "you need to find out who you want to be in the corporate world."

I knew he was right as he continued to speak.

He said, "There are four kinds of people in the corporate workplace."

I was a bit lost; however, I was astute and attentive, hanging onto every word anticipating the enlightenment to be obtained. Coach continued and said, "You have the sacrificial lamb. This is the person who is unaware of the office vibe and the corporate climate. They do just enough, and they are the first to be fired or let go. Then there is the survivalist. This person does his or her job great and goes above board to do a little extra. They are aware of the office climate, and in tune with the company politics and day-to-day operations. They know how to maneuver through corporate ups and downs. Next is the company politician. This person knows everyone and is in everyone's business. This is the ass kisser and the person who brown noses. They are aware of the corporation's direction, climate, take advantage of an opportunity, and they always get promoted based on popularity."

As he spoke, I couldn't help but ponder intensely taking in every word. Things were making sense for the first time.

Lastly, Coach G explained the last corporate person. "The last person is the corporate Machiavelli. This person is the deadliest of the four because this person plays all positions, laughs in people's faces, and then stabs them in the back. This person is a socialite narcissist; they are extremely opportunistic and will do anything to climb the corporate ladder to stay on top at anyone's expense."

Coach G then expounded on why it was imperative that I quickly decide whom I would choose to be because my career and survival would depend on it.

Moving forward, trying to get through classes felt like a challenge and a long, never-ending process. I am sure all college grads can attest to this feeling. I started my college career at eighteen years old, and here I was, attempting to complete the journey toward matriculation at twenty-six years old. I told myself I would complete my bachelor's degree before Barack Obama left office.

In turn, it would not be easy; there were many distractions. I met many new associates and lifetime friends, being from a big city like New York helped a lot with talking to girls and women. I would bed many women throughout my college days at PVAMU, as was the culture of many schools across the nation. Unfortunately, sex, partying, and attending class was how my days went.

I started to gain social traction and built up my confidence in who I was. I did find a college sweetheart at one point in time; her name was Terry. She was from the Bahamas, but I guess what you reap is what you sow, and so I caught her cheating with her ex-boyfriend. So, so much for love, right?

Dating in college taught me a lot about women and my role as a man in a relationship. We had numerous ups and downs, good times, and bad. Then on the early morning of January 30th, 2014, ten days after my 26th birthday would be the worst down point. I was shot in the face while driving down Interstate 290 in Katy, Texas, heading to a hookah bar with Terry. Naturally, you're wondering what happened. I was jamming to some "Soca" music and cruising with my girlfriend when out of nowhere, I felt like I was hit with a one-ton sledgehammer on the left side of my face.

After that, I heard the loud bang and felt the glass of the car window shatter across my face. I immediately felt my head to see if I was shot in my head and to determine if my brains were oozing out or if I was dreaming. As all of this unfolded, I saw my life flash before my eyes. Yes, when you are in shock, your spirit senses the inevitable end of your life. It seemed like an angle altered the bullet, or maybe it was the flash of the bullet leaving the muzzle of the .380 semi-automatic handgun, which I was shot with.

I gained my senses quickly and then swerved into the anonymous, lifted, green pickup truck in which the shooter was driving as if I was in a suspense-filled Denzel Washington movie. To my surprise, he didn't shoot again and instead sped off as I crashed into the side barricade.

After that, I then calmed my girlfriend down who was in total shock, and finally realized that if I didn't get to a hospital, I would bleed out. I am still surprised to this day that I drove myself like Danica Patrick on a racetrack to the nearest hospital with one hand.

This was nothing short of a miracle, of course, Jesus is real, and so I would also need time to heal from the trauma which I experienced and all the police and news investigations. During this time, I went through the process of pledging to become a member of one of the divine nine fraternities, but instead, I would take a leave of absence from school, postpone all endeavors, and head to Trinidad and Tobago.

I felt like I needed to escape, so I took a vacation with my brother, Rueben, to experience a Trinidad carnival and relieve my stress. My mother was in disbelief and still in shock after all of this, but she gave me motherly wisdom. She expressed to me that I should bathe in the sea to help my gunshot wound heal. Ironically, I almost drowned at Maracas beach taking her advice when a strong undercurrent overtook me. My vacation-induced inebriation didn't help things along, but I took this as another life-changing situation.

On a positive note, I had never experienced so much fun in my life. I was supposed to only stay in Trinidad for one week. However, I remained for two weeks. Every day was spent laughing, sharing experiences, and partying to "Soca" day and night. It was socially, emotionally, and mentally healing, a euphoric-like experience altogether.

After my hiatus, I found myself back on task, in school, and focused on working toward the ultimate lifetime goal of graduation. I also faced the reality of overdue school assignments, bills, being a father, and not having a vehicle. So, after in-depth brainstorming, I decided to finance a car since the lemon I had bought broke down one month after the purchase. My dad helped me to finance the car to work part- time as an Uber driver.

I learned yet another invaluable lesson the hard way, which was never to finance a car because it is a depreciating asset. It loses its value as soon as you drive it off the lot or has no worth over time.

I felt that having a car and using it for business purposes would help me to pay off the remaining balance and earn needed money to pay for my bills. Joining Uber would be a daunting and tedious process since I had a felony record for assault. I had to be interviewed several times, see the attorney representing the city of Houston, and prove to a Black woman that I was a reformed citizen who was only trying to obtain my TNC license and needed to drive my car to survive.

After I jumped through all the bureaucratic hurdles and cut through all the red tape, I was finally able to drive for Uber. I worked with Uber for almost two years without an issue and maintained two jobs on campus, in housing and the recreation center. However, life threw me another curveball and wrenched my plans.

One day a deranged guy decided to go on a killing spree in Kalamazoo, Michigan, and in between shooting random people, he decided to pick up Uber customers whom he didn't kill. Well, this affected me by sending major shock waves through the company and ultimately causing Uber to revoke anyone from driving who had a record, including myself. I was netting at least $1500 to $2000 a month, and for a college student, that was considered "bank" or a substantial amount of money to live off. So, Uber dropped me like a hot potato and more or less discriminated against me as most employers do in the United States with people who have a criminal record.

The only thing I could ponder was the conservative cliché, which states, "African American's need to pull themselves up by their bootstraps."

Ironically, we cannot get a job or obtain a loan to create a business to buy the boots, which I deemed as a cruel and hard reality for me to process. Life started to become stressful once again. I was financially overburdened. How was I going to pay my rent and car note with my school jobs? I didn't earn enough.

All this frustration and lack of discipline led me to me walking around with so much tension; this would become evident in having an altercation. I was fired from my campus job for nearly fighting the traffic assistant. So, I parked in the wrong spot twice and was given a fine of $300.

I had to pay my rent, car note, insurance, gas, and buy food. I lost my cool and slapped the ticket machine out of the man's hand. I totally blacked out; I wanted to fight this man. I was honestly stressed out about how my life had been going.

I later turned myself into the campus police and was booked at the county jail on charges of terroristic threats – the same prison in which Sandra Bland was found hanging in her cell several weeks later for a similar dispute with law enforcement.

I went back and forth to court yet again for the umpteenth time in my life. My good friend Bre'von bailed me out of the county jail on a $1000 bond. I was so nerve-wracked and disappointed at myself. In retrospect, I was only one year away from graduation, and I was glad that during this incident I did not physically strike that man. If

I had, I would be in prison for a long time, I would not have graduated, and this book would have never been written.

Not only was I arrested, facing another criminal record, I was also fired from my job as a resident assistant, and now unable to pay my car note. I was homeless. The moral of this incident: I learned that I had to control my emotions, or they will control me and land me jail where they control you.

Once again, I had a trip pre-booked for Miami, Florida, with my brother, Rueben, for a Miami "Soca" Carnival. Instead of fun, I found myself bumping into old enemies from New York City on Ocean Avenue on South Beach. Looking back, I don't know how God allowed me to make it out of Miami and back to Houston, Texas, after running into numerous individuals. The kicker was during my flight back to Houston, and it seemed as if the whole plane was full of old friends turned enemies. I mean, what a strange coincidence, but this was an orchestrated event, and I knew from that day forward once again I couldn't trust anyone. When I landed, I contacted a friend named "Buck" who met me at the airport and escorted me back to Prairie View safely.

From October 2015 to December 2015, my expected graduation date, I did my best to stay on the low, and as an old friend Mike used to say, "Stay out the way."

Here I was still standing after being shot in the face, being hit by a car, surviving prison, completing parole, nearly being killed by fake friends, jobless and homeless. I persevered with the help of my college brother and best friend, Esrom Eyob, who allowed me to sleep on the floor and live rent-free for almost two years. I found jobs through 1099 contracts for various experiential marketing companies for the next year. After all the ups and downs and the inertia of life, I finally faced the finish line and was several months away from almost a decade-long goal of finally walking across that stage to obtain my degree.

Surely, gaining and transferring in twenty-four credits, which I garnered by going to community college all those years earlier and even enrolling in Marist College while incarcerated, allowed me to speed up this process of matriculating a whole year ahead of my degree plan. As you can imagine, my life as an adolescent, teenager, and young adult leading up until that very moment was like a rollercoaster that never stopped going down. Sometimes it felt like a suspense thriller or better yet as if a 300-pound gorilla of fear, pressure, and expectation was on my back. These tumultuous feelings led me to contemplate suicide several times throughout life, but at this particular moment, I felt relieved and proud of myself.

God allowed me to survive the constant ups and downs which at times were self-inflicted, and sometimes just life throwing trials and tribulations. On December 12th, 2015, at 11:00 a.m. God allowed me to finally walk across the stage of the Prairie View A&M University stage to join the Class of Fall 2015 for the graduation commencement. I completed my ten-year college journey with a Bachelor of Science in Human Performance, with honors, and above a 3.0-grade point average. As I sat in my seat during the honorary ceremony of my commencement, I could not help but think about life up until this very point; I could feel that gorilla of social pressure vanished from my shoulders.

Here I was after all the mistakes, mess ups and dark times, finally completing college with my parents and loyal comrades in attendance as well as my friend, Ms. Iscah, watching from home via the internet. This moment allowed tears of joy to flow down my face. If you have ever graduated from college or reached a long-desired goal, you will understand the amount of joy that overwhelmed me. I was filled with delight, disbelief, relief, satisfaction, and it was hard to hold back all of these emotions.

Let's be real for a moment. I mean, what are the odds of a little Black boy from the inner city of New York who was expelled from over fourteen different schools, placed in special education, suspended multiple times, received a G.E.D, was incarcerated, had a son, survived several near-death experiences including being shot in the face during a shooting spree being able to graduate? Who, having lived in the valley and walked in the shadow of death would emerge victorious through all of those challenges to matriculate from one of the oldest Black universities in the United States.

Jesus allowed me to get to this very junction; of walking proudly across the stage once hearing my name being summoned by the announcer. It felt like I was dreaming, and I still feel like I am sometimes dreaming. The truth is I finally completed the goal which I had set out to achieve over eight years ago at my local junior college.

Although numerous naysayers expressed to me time and time again, "With a felony, you cannot become a physical education teacher," I still went forward anyway, and I am glad I did. I say all of that to say to you don't ever let some poor negative energy or words of negative discouragement into your life, especially if it is meant to hinder you from your purpose.

The burden which was lifted came in the form of relief from the social pressure that had existed before graduating from college. I felt so much anxiety from my past failures, also not being able to meet superficial societal standards, and from causing my family so much shame and pain. This achievement was going to make amends for all of that and more – this would be my right of social, economic, financial, and redemption passage.

Nevertheless, December 12th, 2015, came and went, and the reality of life after college started to present challenge after challenge, a constant uphill, daily grind of the rat race was now my new social dilemma. This is where the rubber meets the road as the adage says; for me I was facing the hard truth, while working a part-time job (Just Over Broke) at a local hospital earning only $12 an hour. I sure did apply to other jobs, I filled out dozens upon dozens of applications and went on countless interviews.

In my mind, I figured that corporations would not only see my criminal record but that they would weigh it against my accomplishments since that time, especially my education and community involvement. Statistically, I had done the impossible: I stayed out of prison, stopped hanging on the streets with gangsters, changed my environment, stopped using drugs, and graduated from college with a high G.P.A.

The cold reality was that I followed the textbook for change. Still, society's outlook in America regarding a person or people with a criminal record, also a minority and one with an advanced degree was still the same. In essence, you're either overqualified (new jargon) or disqualified due to one of the reasons above.

My worst fear was starting to come to fruition, and maybe this was the art of seduction and the laws of attraction at play. Before going back to school, as I drove down the street in my work van, I recalled myself saying that I would never invest thousands of dollars on a piece a paper from a university. Well, I ended up eating my words, and I did just that, but the underlying reason was that I had a grave outlook on higher education due to some factors. Once I wasn't sure what I would major in, I lacked academic confidence, and finally, because I was afraid of taking such a financial gamble to find myself in the position which I was in.

I was now educated according to the traditional societal standard, after having spent nearly $40,000 on undergraduate and another $40,000 on graduate school. I still was unable to acquire suitable employment to pay my bills due to my past mistakes before returning to school.

I took a loan, I remained studious, sacrificed being around my family and friends for the past several years, just to be faced with such a stressful and discouraging dilemma. I volunteered as a firefighter throughout my undergraduate degree. I joined community organizations, and I worked as many odd jobs as could find so that I could have a chance at gaining a position within the corporate sector once I matriculated. Unfortunately, the reality was I would – and will – always be labeled a criminal or judged as such in the court of public opinion.

This kind of mindset caused me to experience extreme bias and prejudices. It is super difficult being an African American male in America. Then, you add your past mistakes and becoming educated. These circumstances make you socially enigmatic, in other words, a threat. Most expect people to stay stagnant and the same in such instances; no benefit of the doubt is given to the idea of change, or reform, revamp and make a genuine three-hundred-and-sixty-degree change forthe better.

The reality is that many folks don't want African Americans to improve, let alone young Black men, and in many cases, the ones close to you don't want to see you do better.

MOVING ON UP

decided to continue moving forward in a positive direction and stay persistent. I did work at the hospital part-time for sixteen months, and I finally saved enough money to move out of my college roommate's house, where I had been sleeping on the floor and couch for almost two years. I was bumming it for a while; now, I had finally found my apartment, my vehicle, this meant more bills and responsibilities.

Most days I spent brainstorming about how I could move up in the company. I didn't understand how people could work so hard and remain complacent in one position. The truth was although I had a job, I was still earning way below the poverty line. I was poor and broke financially, but rich in spirit. So, I decided to change course and enroll back in school to pursue my firefighting career since I volunteered for three years while pursuing my undergraduate degree.

Before this, several months earlier, I had passed the Houston Fire Department test. However, I declined the intake process as it required me to quit school in October and I would graduate that

December. Now, I was once again trying to pursue a career which I enjoyed, even before I entered fire school at Houston Community College.

I applied to the Texas Commission Fire Protection and was denied by a conservative White gentleman named Mr. Jim Humphreys. He stated that the administrative law of Texas would not yield or allow a person with a felony record to become a commissioned firefighter. I was told "no" most of my life.

I couldn't find a decent full-time job, so I thought, *what do I have to lose enrolling?* So, I enrolled in the firefighting course and completed the 26-week course, which was physically and mentally draining. I started in January 2016 and graduated the summer of that year after countless days in the Texas summer heat.

One day, while attending school, I was given pain and punishment (disciplinary action). I was required to walk two miles in 100 pounds of firefighting bunker gear while carrying a fire hose roll. I know you are asking, what did I do now? Basically, I was being a hard head and not following instructions.

Moving forward, I excelled through my classes and I passed the Texas Fire Fighting level one and two state exams. After this significant milestone, I felt that I could have a chance at becoming a certified firefighter. Unfortunately, reality set in, and my desires, along with my willingness, would not be enough to get me into the fire service in Texas.

All my life, people had been naysayers. Companies had discriminated against me with their anti-conviction policies and, in turn, had subliminally tried to crush my aspirations. I have come to learn and deal with this kind of cynical, predisposed pessimism wrapped in political and legal bureaucratic rhetoric by staying persistent and allowing my self-education to cut through all this systematic red tape.

The final decision from the state of Texas was that I would not be able to be commissioned as a certified firefighter. What a crushing blow after all the money and hard work I put in. I felt distraught due to the rejection and, more importantly, the time spent going to school, I missed out on numerous job opportunities.

Throughout all this, I realized that I would never be able to shake the systematic social stigmatism of being a felon in the United States. Although I had the drive and ambition, it did not seem to be helping me to stay afloat. I found myself desperate and hungry for any opportunity.

As the old saying goes, everything happens for a reason. At this point, I could not seem to see the reasoning or why I couldn't be given a chance to pursue a meaningful career. In desperation to find a better job (JUST Over Broke), or position in someone's corporation, I quit my job at the hospital to try to work for an at-home company. The company appeared to be legit and I was interviewed via the phone. In the coming weeks, I faced one of the hardest realities yet. The company turned out to be fake. I was at my emotional and financial breaking point, and I came to an end where I even contemplated suicide, which wasn't the first time I thought about such a thing, but I am not a quitter.

My rent was due, my car note was three months behind, and I had no more money for food. Thanks to my parents, I found yet another financial or economic stimulus package for the hundredth time.

RETROSPECTION

I had to look myself in the mirror and conduct meaningful introspection because I was all out of options. I did just that and thought about what I truly enjoyed doing the most.

What were the things I loved the most? I concluded it was traveling. It was something I have always loved but never really been able to explore due to my life circumstances. So, I made it my job, day and night, from October 2016 to search for jobs that would pay me to travel and, most importantly, compensate me for my time.

After two weeks of searching the internet, I discovered teaching abroad in foreign countries, and so I applied to numerous jobs.

I landed a recruiter named Tom, who was a fast-talking Italian guy from New Jersey; he almost persuaded me to sign a contract with a school in a not-so-good part of China.

From that point forward, I did more and more research, and in doing so, I discovered a young lady on *YouTube* by the name of

Unique Travels. I decided to get in contact with this young lady through emails and social media, and she would be my guiding light throughout my process of finding a job in Asia.

I applied to many positions, and several companies reached out to me, specifically from China. It seemed impossible to conduct interviews on Skype and Chinese applications such as *WeChat*. I found myself meeting several people online before going to China, which is where I would relocate after all this time.

I found a job teaching kids in China. I signed a contract making more than I was making in the United States, and from that point, I would also receive help from the school and several other sources to secure my visa and proper living arrangements. My parents helped me to purchase my plane ticket to China on a one-way trip.

The reality of all these new happenings wouldn't set in until I found myself donating and giving away most of my clothes to the local Goodwill. I had no idea what lay ahead, but the ball was rolling. I applied for a new passport. I terminated my lease agreement, donated my belongings, and put my soon-to-be repossessed car in a storage unit.

The time to leave America and all I knew came quicker than I had anticipated. That day I took an Uber to the airport, cleared customs, and barely made it in time for my first flight to Seattle, Washington, where I would connect to a flight to China.

My layover in Seattle would be my last night on American soil for a long time, which I didn't realize at that point. I found myself searching Google for local restaurants once I arrived at my hotel. I found a bar, and although the kitchen was closed, the bartender was kind enough to have the cook make some chicken tenders for me.

After that, we chatted about where I was hailing from, and where I was headed. She was amazed and even offered me a ride back to my hotel since it was super late. This lady was another blessing in disguise, or better put, another angel I encountered along my life's path, and this would be my only experience in the rainy city of Seattle, Washington.

That night I could not sleep much since my mind was restless. I was filled with mixed emotions. I asked myself over and over what am I doing? Was this the right thing to do?

Before leaving Texas, I asked God for a sign to see if heading to Asia was the right decision. Well, I needed to record a basketball coaching video as a demo for a potential position. As I walked into the local Y.M.C.A., there were several Asian kids playing basketball; they willingly volunteered to record a coaching session for free. This was the go-ahead sign which I was looking for, and all that was left was to take a 7,000-mile leap of faith and see the outcome.

I made it to the Seattle airport with plenty of time, ready to board a plane to a foreign land called China. I had only read of this place and seen it in numerous over-exaggerated movies, but today this would be my destination. The visual stereotypes were rampant inside of my cranium of all the Jackie Chan and Bruce Lee movies. I thought about all the possibilities, dirt roads, people with rice hats, or even of all the *YouTube* videos of Chinese bad habits. I watched several videos about the land of fake goods, also known as China, and how they make fake handbags to counterfeit eggs. I even envisioned militia parading through the streets like the Nazi communist party or the government playing propaganda over the city's P.A. system like Stalin in Russia.

This was my longest flight ever, which consisted of sixteen long hours to Shanghai. My level of anxiety had never been so high, especially as I looked around the plane and saw no other African American faces. That's when the reality set in once again that I was journeying to another part of the world, alone, and filled with mixed emotions. I was going to a place where customs were different from mine, and the food and language were also different.

Anyone who has lived abroad can attest to the level of excitement when going to a new place, leaving your last destination to a new one, especially America – the fantasy land of opportunity where the streets are paved with goals and the land of free speech, freedom of expression, and multiple cultures. There I was trading it in for totalitarianism and opportunity in a faraway land.

Well, after several rare cognacs, sleeping, and movies, I finally arrived at Pudong International Airport. Having cleared customs and gathered my things, I finally realized that I was now on Chinese soil—the home of fake handbags, stinky tofu, Confucius, and the home of the Great Wall.

The first person I met was my new company's liaison after searching and waiting for an hour due my lack of a Chinese sim card, which I had to purchase. The young Chinese lady's name was "Bella," and she had the hugest forehead that I had ever seen, just making jokes.

The ride from the airport was one of the longest I have ever taken in my life and was filled with me recording videos and taking pictures of the new country I was in. The taxi driver or "Shifu" as it is called drove like the old video game *Crazy Taxi*; it was insane, crazy lane changes, lack of signaling, and oh the occasional stomping of the breaks. The irony was that everyone seemed to drive equally horribly, if not worse, on top of the outlandish honking for every little thing.

After hours in the back of that cab, I arrived at a dilapidated hotel, the equivalent of a Motel 6 in America. The hotel smelled like cigarettes and mold from the moment you entered the establishment. My nose and senses were being bombarded by scents which I have never encountered in my entire existence, not even in prison. This was a struggle for me. I felt like a hiker on Mount Everest regarding how hard it was trying to breathe; the air was thick with pollution and smoke. This was a sobering reminder that I was no longer in the comforts of America, or as put directly from the famous classic movie the *Wizard of OZ*, "You're not in Kansas anymore!"

I would be housed in this subpar hotel for two weeks. Every night was frigid and cold like a Christmas night in New York City. On top of this experience was the new journey to find food. I had to survive by eating dumplings and McDonalds, which caused me to gain a tremendous amount of weight.

After that, I found a modern apartment and that reshaped my perception of China. I had amenities and a modern kitchen. This was a better apartment than the one I had in America and a bit less expensive than the rent I was paying back in Texas.

Now that I had my living situation and food sort of handled, it was time to do what I had migrated to China to do – Work! My job was going to be to teach children English. When I was stateside, I figured how hard could this be? Well, I was in for a surprise; the company was utterly disorganized. I attended training for several days and then was put in a classroom to teach kids that ranged from three to twelve years old. If you have never worked with a three- or four-year-old, it can be a rude awakening. It is hard to teach them how to sit still and learn, especially if they think you are a scary person or a big piece of chocolate as many kids thought by trying to lick me or touch my skin.

Basically, I was to teach the kids full-on immersion of the English language mixed with clowning for the entertainment of the kids and parents. I worked like a slave twenty hours on the weekend from 9:00 a.m. to 8:00 p.m. My feet and body hurt from the standing and dancing, and my voice most days was dead after the ten hours of the talking and yelling.

The job was mentally taxing and the administration was very demanding, so I started to search for better work after seven months of some of the most mentally draining work. As Jay-Z once said, "If you can make it here (NYC), you can make it anywhere." Right? More importantly, this was officially my first full-time corporate job after graduating from college.

I resigned after seven long months and found a new job working at a Chinese high school called Jin Cai in Pudong China. This school also had its pros and cons. Therefore, I realized quickly that China was no different from the American corporation machine or the bureaucratic bull regarding workplace issues and politics. I learned quickly that Chinese people, administrators, are lazy and disorganized, which is a total contradiction to what we are taught in American culture. So, experiencing the country and people firsthand was a total epiphany, as well as an extreme culture shock for me in that it taught me to appreciate certain aspects of my upbringing, my parent's wisdom and to be proud of character attributes which I possessed and took for granted, e.g., work ethic.

I was employed at a Chinese high school and finally achieved the goal of gaining a position for what I went to school for, a Physical Education teacher. My first year teaching didn't go so well at the first two schools. The school did not provide health checks for the students, and one girl had an asthma attack. On that day, I argued with two teachers about their conduct. I quickly realized as my mentor and manager, Mike Washington, would bluntly put it, "You are a hired gun, and this isn't a real school, this is the hospital."

Mike helped me to refocus my mental and emotional equity; he helped me to home in what was more important, which were my goals. So, I did just that, I enrolled back in school in October 2017 at the American Military University to pursue a degree in Sports Management. I ironed out a five-year plan to clean up my credit (fix my financial house), save money, and ultimately purchase my first piece of real estate. Furthermore, as my manager, Mike encouraged me to apply to another school, which had fewer requirements and allowed me more freedom to complete the goals above, while keeping the bills paid. I am currently halfway through my master's program, and my consumer debt is paid off.

My life has been nothing short of eventful and full of interesting happenings, but I must say that what has helped me is the ability to be self-taught. You may be asking, what do you mean by this notion of self-education? As I continued to search for solutions to help me improve and grow spiritually, socially, financially, and economically, I discovered a few strategies, which I will share with you to help improve your life as the reader. The strategies I discovered were self-acceptance, self-accountability, self-help, a mentor, and a healthy desire to grow in all aspects of your life. Now, let me explain how I applied each of these strategies to my life.

I had to accept myself as a person who was imperfect yet with a desire to do better, to be better. This meant I had to conduct, and I continue to perform, introspection while constantly assessing my life. By doing so, you allow yourself to reflect on your life in retrospect and also to envision where you see yourself in the future.

Self-accountability is the ability to correct yourself and to be responsible for all your actions. I have discovered that this skill requires a lot of discipline. One way to help hold myself accountable was to surround myself with a new circle of friends who would have no problem reminding me that I have to take responsibility for my actions, my conduct, my finances, economics, and my health.

I have solely consumed self-help in the form of reading books on the rich, real estate, strategies, and motivation. For instance, take a look at the following books:

• "The Millionaire Next Door" by Thomas J. Stanley and William D. Danko taught me not to keep up with everyone else.

• Another beneficial book was "Think and Grow Rich" by Napoleon Hill, which showed me how to think and conceptualize what I want out of life.

• "Investing in Rental Properties for Beginners" by Lisa Phillips showed me that anyone with a particular strategy can buy and sell real estate.

• "The Communist Manifesto" by Carl Marx explained communism which helped me to contrast America's government format and to learn the pros and cons of both as a worker and consumer.

• "The Personal MBA" by Josh Kaufman is where I learned how to assess businesses.

• "Who Moved My Cheese" by Spencer Johnson reminded me that staying in place and not changing is dangerous and can hinder growth.

- "The Secret to Success" by Eric Thomas allowed me to understand that I would have to sacrifice many things to become successful.

- "Rich Dad Poor Dad" by Robert T. Kiyosaki explained the different schools of thought when it came to money and wealth – the poor view money one way and the rich view it as a way to make more money.

- "How an Economy Grows and Why it Crashes" by Peter Schiff and Andrew Schiff explained the ins and outs of how economies work, which is critical to understand as a consumer.

I have also read hundreds of articles on various topics ranging from business to self-help. I truly believe that information is only powerful if used. I desire to be a better person and to become extremely successful; therefore, I feel it is my duty to ensure this through self-education and formal education.

THE FINAL COUNTDOWN

Throughout this book, I expounded on many people who had a positive impact on my life and who have tremendously helped me. The importance of having a real-time, living example of what you're trying to accomplish in the form of a role model is priceless.

Mentors are like beacons of hope and brilliant examples of what to do and what not to do; they can allow you to express your ideas and critique them in love. They will also be there to help you to avoid costly and timely mistakes. Do your best to find a mentor, whether it is at your local place of worship, in your family, community via volunteer opportunities, or by joining an organization of like-minded people such as Lions Clubs International or Rotary International.

A healthy desire to grow is going to be the mental engine that you will need to capitalize on any of these strategies the way I have. You may have all of these strategies down pat, but you will need divine intervention and strength from the Lord to succeed ultimately. Your desire is the will to persist no matter what. This is the tenacity to continue toward your goals when everyone is telling you no or when challenge after challenge continue once you conquered one. I genuinely hope that you can use these strategies and others that you may discover along your life journey, which can help you to succeed.

The point of this story is everyone has a purpose in life and God has given me ample chances to change course and head in a direction such as the one I am pursuing. I want to humbly say that it is only by the grace of God through Jesus Christ that I can produce the story in which I have written for you to read. I hope that no matter who you are this book has allowed you to see that Christ can not only change a person but also that you can'tdoitalone.Ihopethat this book will encourage and show young people who have challenges that anything is possible with faith in Jesus Christ and hard work. Thank you for reading my story, and I pray that my story will inspire you to greatness.

ABOUT THE AUTHOR

My name is Jonmarc Lenn Dewalt, and I am thirty-two years old. I was born in Manhattan, New York, and raised in St. Albans, Queens, New York. I wrote this book to share my story of what it was like growing up in a lower-middle-class neighborhood and living in two parallel worlds. I have been incarcerated, shot, assaulted, racially profiled and dealt with many more unfortunate circumstances.

I managed to turn my life around for the greater good. I graduated from a historically Black University, Prairie View A&M University with a Bachelor of Science degree and obtained my Masters in Sports Management from the American Military University. I also received my Firefighting Certification from Houston Community College and I have gone on to receive a teaching license from the Utah Board of Education. I served my community as a Volunteer Firefighter for over three years, and I am continuing to better myself via counseling and self-education. My hobbies include basketball, karate, reading on real estate and investing, cooking, and traveling the world. This is a story of truth and redemption, how people can do well, and reach their full God-given potential when given a second chance.

Thank you for purchasing my book. If you would be ever so kind and leave me an honest review on Amazon and my Goodreads page.